THE ART OF TAROT GUIDEBOOK

Copyright © 2025 by Tam Dillon
All rights reserved. No part of this book may be reproduced in any manner whatsoever without written permission except in the case of brief quotations embodied in critical articles and reviews.
Current edition, third

First edition, released 2019
Second edition, released 2021
Third edition, released 2025

Publisher: The Peacock and The Owl

The Art of Tarot Guidebook

TAM DILLON

Contents

Preface ix
Introduction xiii

1. The Fundamentals of Tarot — 1
2. The Practical Aspects — 7
3. Interpreting the Tarot — 15
4. Uses for the Tarot — 23
5. Questioning the Tarot — 31
6. Understanding Spreads — 39
7. The Three Traditions — 61
8. Tarot Through the Sephirotic Tree — 73
9. The Major Arcana — 89
10. The Minor Arcana — 137
11. The Court Cards — 173
12. Card Associations — 187
13. Intuition Development — 203
14. Oracle Cards — 211

About Tam Dillon 217

Dedication

FOR JADIE,

Thank you for placing the cards in my hands all those years ago. It was an honor to have you as my first Tarot teacher. Your journey here has ended, big brother. Rest easy now, your wisdom and teachings live on.

You were a true Tarot Master.

Preface

My journey with Tarot began more than twenty years ago when my older brother Jadie introduced me to the cards. Jadie was my first and most influential Tarot teacher, someone I admired both as a reader and as a mentor. When I wrote the first edition of this guidebook, I was honored to have him proofread it. I still remember the moment he told me, "I would have loved a book like this when I first started out with the cards. It would have made my journey so much simpler." Those words meant a great deal to me then and still do.

When working with Tarot, my focus has always been on keeping it simple. This guidebook was never meant to overcomplicate the process of reading the cards. Instead, it was written to help people build confidence in their ability to read Tarot, trust their intuition and understand the cards in a way that is practical and useful.

Jadie passed away as I was finalizing the second edition of this book and was unable to proofread it or give me his nod of approval, but I know with certainty that it would have made him proud. That second edition went on to become my best seller, reinforcing the importance of making Tarot accessible to those who want to learn. This third edition refines that goal even further.

X ~ *PREFACE*

Since the release of the previous edition, my work with Tarot has evolved. In 2019, I retired from traditional Tarot readings to focus on education and deeper self-exploration through the cards. I initially stepped away from offering readings entirely, believing that my role was solely as a teacher. It wasn't until 2023 that I recognized the opportunity to integrate my experience as a reader with my work in self-development coaching. This realization led me to develop a different approach to readings - one that does not focus on answering specific questions, but instead provides insights into aspects of a person that they may not see for themselves.

This shift in focus is reflected in the third edition of this book. The content remains as practical and user-friendly as ever, but with expanded insights into card themes and imagery, numerology, Tarot spreads and the role of Oracle cards. The Fundamentals section has been restructured to allow for a more natural learning progression and additional insight has been added to support intuitive development.

Jadie was a gifted reader and teacher. Much of what I know and understand about Tarot comes from the knowledge he shared, the books and decks he introduced me to and the countless conversations we had about the cards, the occult and the wisdom found in ancient traditions. I am the Tarot reader and teacher I am today because he put a deck of cards in my hands more than twenty years ago and said, "You need to check these out. They're awesome and I think they'll suit you nicely."

PREFACE ~ XI

That moment set me on a path of exploration that continues to this day. Tarot is a tool that evolves with you, deepens your self-awareness and reflects back what you need to see. Whether you are picking up a deck for the first time or looking to strengthen your understanding of the cards, I hope this book helps you develop a practice that is both insightful and empowering.

Introduction

To understand the purpose of Tarot, it helps to first understand what Tarot is. At its core, it is a set of picture cards used predominantly for divination and self-development. Divination is the act of seeking guidance, making it clear that Tarot is not about predicting the future, but rather about providing insight that guides one toward their future. From a self-development perspective, Tarot serves as a tool for self-awareness, personal insight and spiritual growth. It provides a structured way to explore one's inner landscape, recognize patterns and gain clarity on challenges and decisions.

The Tarot reflects a symbolic path of transformation - one that aligns with the esoteric teachings found in ceremonial magic, ancient cultures and various occult traditions. The cards illustrate the natural cycles of personal growth, mirroring the phases of learning, struggle and mastery that shape a person's evolution. They have been used for centuries by seekers, scholars and mystics to deepen their understanding of themselves and the world around them.

This book is designed to shed light on how you can work with Tarot from both perspectives - divination and self-development - as each offers immense value. While divination seeks guidance from external sources, self-development through Tarot is an internal process, using the cards as a reflective tool for deeper understanding. Tarot is more than a system of card meanings; it is a practical tool for self-inquiry, transformation and alignment.

This third edition expands on these aspects, providing additional spreads, deeper insights into symbols and more practical applications for working with the cards - whether for personal exploration, intuitive readings or structured guidance.

The Origins of Tarot — From Divination to Self-Development

The use of Tarot for divination began with Jean-Baptiste Alliette, Anton de Gebelin and the Tarot de Marseille - a popular deck in the late 1700s. You may know Jean-Baptiste by his pen name, Etteilla, a name still found on published works today. Etteilla was the first professional, paid card reader and the author of the first book on how to use playing cards for divination. He also assigned divinatory meanings to the four suits, shaping how Tarot would later be interpreted. According to Etteilla, he was taught the art of card reading by a cartomancer from Piedmont, Italy, and he later shared these teachings in his works.

Anton de Gebelin further expanded the world of cartomancy by connecting Tarot to Ancient Egyptian wisdom in *Le Monde Primitif*, proposing that the cards contained the original teachings of Thoth - the Egyptian god of knowledge. Etteilla built on these theories, developing Tarot into the divinatory tool we recognize today. Over time, the teachings of Thoth evolved into the teachings of Hermes Trismegistus, and Tarot as a tool for structured insight was shaped by Hermetic orders and prominent occultists.

Alongside divination, Tarot was being structured around self-development and initiation. The word revelation comes from reveal, which is the foundation of this approach - the journey of uncovering one's true self and nature. Some of the most well-known figures in this lineage are Arthur Edward Waite and Aleister Crowley. A.E. Waite, with the artistic collaboration of Pamela Colman Smith, created what is now the most widely used Tarot system - the Smith-Waite tradition. Most modern decks follow this structure. Crowley, in the late 1930s, worked with Lady Frieda Harris to develop the second major tradition in Tarot - the Thoth tradition.

During this time, Tarot became intertwined with Kabbalah, the twenty-two letters of the Hebrew alphabet and the Sephirotic Tree. This is explored in some depth later in this guidebook. It was also aligned with spiritual alchemy and the process of reaching the Philosopher's Stone. Many Hermetic orders incorporated the cards into their initiations and teachings, embedding ancient wisdom within their symbolism. These foundations remain strong today, even as new insights and interpretations continue to emerge. The core purpose has remained consistent - Tarot as a guide for empowerment, authenticity and self-awareness.

Tarot has evolved over centuries, with three main traditions influencing its structure and symbolism. While there are three primary traditions - *De Marseille*, Waite-Smith and Thoth - this book follows the Waite-Smith system as its foundation. This is due to it being the most widely recognized and accessible system, used in the majority of modern decks. It was the first deck to fully illustrate the Minor Arcana, making for more intuitive interpretation through imagery. The Three Traditions section provides an overview of the *De Marseille* and Crowley's Thoth systems, giving insight into how they differ.

Working with Tarot

Tarot can seem overwhelming at first. You may have preconceptions or even feel intimidated by the cards, but there's nothing to fear – in reality, they're just a pack of cards. The real knowledge and power comes from the person reading them. Tarot is a tool for learning and self-exploration, and the process is always an internal one.

If you're unsure where to start, start where you are. If you've never picked up a deck before, begin by pulling a card and taking a look. If you've been reading for years, revisit your cards and explore them from a fresh perspective. It doesn't matter how or where you begin - just start.

Why should you start? Because guidance is something we all seek. The practice of divination has existed for centuries, and humans have always looked for ways to understand themselves and the world better. Learning to use a tool like Tarot for guidance and self-development isn't as daunting as it might seem when approached with the right perspective. Knowing why you want to work with the cards and what motivates you to learn them is essential.

Everyone's intention for learning Tarot is different. Ask yourself why you want to learn to read the cards. Understanding your intention will help guide your path and give you direction. Your reason for learning doesn't have to be static either. My own approach to the cards has shifted many times over the years. I recommend regularly checking in with your intentions.

Knowing why you read helps refine your questions and maintain a healthy relationship with your practice. It's easy to develop an unhealthy reliance on the cards - reading out of desperation for answers, for example, often results in muddled interpretations. Reading from a space of anxiety, panic or overthinking will cloud your judgment. Tarot is best read with clarity, not emotional attachment. While the cards can explore emotional aspects, readings themselves should not come from an emotionally charged state. The same applies to intellectualizing - read with intuition, not pure reasoning.

Intuition is Everything

Intuition is the ability to know something without conscious reasoning - you just know. This is the foundation of reading Tarot. You cannot work with the cards without using your intuition. Even the simple act of drawing a card is an intuitive one; something led you to pull a card in the first place.

Your intuition influences everything you do. The more in tune you are with yourself, the clearer your readings will be. This is why Tarot is so effective for self-awareness and personal growth

- it strengthens your ability to trust your inner knowing. If you struggle to connect with your intuition or don't fully understand how it works, don't worry. There is an entire section later in this book dedicated to developing it further.

Updates in this Edition

With this third edition, I have further refined the way I present Tarot. I have expanded on its transformative applications, deepened the card association pages, added additional symbols and references, and included new spreads and example readings. My approach to Tarot has also evolved - I now integrate it more deeply into my self-development coaching and Tarot Therapy sessions, helping people understand their patterns, experiences and areas of growth in a more structured way.

Right, enough talk. If you take one thing from this guidebook, let it be this - keep it simple.

Now, let's get into learning some Tarot as you travel light as the Fool, equipped with the tools of the Magician and the wisdom of the High Priestess.

Tam Dillon
Tarot Master

Chapter 1

The Fundamentals of Tarot

What the Tarot Is and Isn't

Tarot is often misunderstood. Some see it as a mystical tool for fortune-telling, while others dismiss it as mere superstition. The truth is, Tarot is neither of these things. It is a structured system of imagery and symbols that reflect the patterns and archetypes of human experience.

At its core, Tarot is a tool for insight, self-reflection and guidance. It does not tell the future, but offers perspectives that help navigate present circumstances. The cards act as mirrors, revealing the energies at play and highlighting possibilities based on one's current path.

Tarot is a language of symbols. Every card carries imagery that speaks to universal themes - cycles of growth, transition, challenge and transformation. Whether used for personal exploration or to help others gain clarity, Tarot's effectiveness comes from its ability to make the unseen visible.

Understanding how Tarot works means letting go of the idea that it provides fixed answers. It is not about fate being predetermined, but about awareness. The more you engage with the cards, the more you see them as a framework for decision-making, pattern recognition and deepening self-awareness.

Origins of Tarot

Historically, Tarot has been used in two primary ways - as a tool for divination and as a system for self-development. While these approaches overlap, they serve different purposes.

Divination is the practice of seeking insight through external means. In Tarot, this involves interpreting the cards as messages that reveal possibilities, patterns or hidden influences. This method does not predict a fixed future, but provides clarity on current energies and potential outcomes.

The use of Tarot for divination became widely recognized in the 18th century with figures like Jean-Baptiste Alliette, known as Etteilla, and Antoine Court de Gébelin, who introduced structured meanings to the cards. They connected Tarot to mystical teachings, including Egyptian wisdom and the idea that the cards held hidden knowledge of the universe.

Over time, Tarot evolved beyond divination and became a self-development tool. Figures like A. E. Waite and Aleister Crowley saw Tarot as a system of transformation, linked to psychology, alchemy and spiritual growth. Rather than looking for answers outside oneself, this approach encourages deep self-exploration, helping us recognize our patterns, behaviours and potential for growth.

Both perspectives - divination and self-development - offer valuable ways to work with the cards. Some use Tarot for guidance, others for reflection and many blend both approaches.

Using Tarot For Self Awareness & Personal Growth

Tarot acts as a mirror for the subconscious. It helps reveal thoughts, emotions and dynamics that may not be immediately obvious. When used intentionally, it becomes a tool for gaining deeper self-awareness, improving decision-making and fostering natural personal growth.

Some ways Tarot can support self-development include -

- Identifying personal patterns and recognizing recurring themes in your life and relationships
- Exploring emotional and mental states to gain clarity and insight on fears, motivations and desires
- Developing intuition and strengthening trust in your inner voice
- Processing change and transition to understand challenges and navigate transformation
- Using Tarot in journaling as a prompt for personal insights and breakthroughs

Unlike traditional divination, self-development Tarot does not seek external guidance, but helps the reader better understand the inner workings of the self. It is a method of self-inquiry that encourages curiosity and honest self-reflection.

Understanding Tarot's Core Structure

Tarot is structured into two main sections - the major arcana and minor arcana - each serving a unique purpose in readings. Together, these sections create a layered system of meaning, allowing for both practical and deep insights. Understanding how they interact is essential to reading Tarot effectively.

The major arcana consists of twenty-two cards representing significant life lessons, archetypal energies and deep transformation. These cards illustrate the key stages of personal growth and evolution, from the Fool's beginning to the World's completion. They do not focus on everyday events but instead highlight major transitions and universal experiences. When a reading contains multiple major arcana cards, it often suggests that the situation at hand is deeply impactful, with long-term significance.

The minor arcana consists of fifty-six cards that provide insight into daily life, thoughts, emotions and challenges. These cards are divided into four suits, each representing a different aspect of experience:

- **Wands** – Passion, creativity, action and ambition
- **Cups** – Emotions, relationships, intuition and connections

- **Swords** – Thoughts, challenges, intellect and communication
- **Pentacles** – Material world, career, stability and physical reality

Each suit contains ten numbered cards (Ace through Ten) and four court cards (Page, Knight, Queen, and King). The numbered cards illustrate different stages of personal experiences, while the court cards often represent personality traits, roles or specific influences within a situation.

Where the major arcana speaks to overarching life themes, the minor arcana expands on the details, showing how these larger themes play out in everyday circumstances.

The Role of Duality in Tarot

An essential aspect of Tarot's structure is duality. Every card contains both a light and a shadow aspect - opposing yet complementary forces. This duality is present throughout Tarot, from the balance of major and minor arcana to the contrast within individual cards.

For example, the Sun represents joy, clarity and success, but in certain contexts, it may highlight overconfidence or a superficial view of happiness. The Moon, on the other hand, is often associated with intuition and mystery, but it can also indicate uncertainty or illusion. This interplay of meanings ensures that Tarot reflects life's complexity rather than offering simplistic answers.

Similarly, the suits of the minor arcana also have their dual natures. Wands' energy can be inspiring and full of movement, but it can also lead to impulsiveness or burnout. Swords bring clarity and intellect but can also signify overthinking or conflict. Recognizing this balance allows for a deeper understanding of the cards.

Working with Tarot's Structure

Tarot's structure is designed to offer layers of meaning. When reading, paying attention to the balance of major and minor arcana in a spread can provide insight into the nature of the situation.

- A reading dominated by major arcana cards suggests deep life shifts and long-term influence.
- A reading with mostly minor arcana cards focuses on everyday events, personal actions and current challenges.
- A strong presence of one suit may indicate a theme - such as a reading full of Cups pointing to emotional matters or a reading with many Swords highlighting mental processes and decisions.

Each card in Tarot serves a purpose, and its position in a spread, alongside its interaction with other cards, shapes the overall interpretation. Tarot is not meant to be read in isolation but as a connected system where meaning emerges from the relationships between the cards.

Chapter 2

The Practical Aspects

Tarot as a Tool for Self-Reflection

Tarot is not about predicting what will happen, but about reflecting on what is already happening. The cards serve as a tool to help bring subconscious thoughts, emotions and patterns into awareness. They offer a structured way to explore personal experiences, clarify challenges and gain insight into decisions.

Each card contains layers of meaning, and through reflection, new understandings emerge. A reading is not about getting answers from an outside source but about recognizing what is already present within. The imagery, symbolism and structure of the cards provide a framework for contemplation, guiding you toward a deeper understanding of your inner world.

I am a big advocate for the practice of journaling, particularly when it comes to the Tarot. Journaling can be a valuable way to work with Tarot as a reflective tool. Writing about card meanings, personal interpretations and the emotions and thoughts that arise in readings allows for deeper processing. Over time, patterns begin to emerge, showing how experiences evolve and how your personal growth unfolds.

Tarot is most effective when approached with curiosity rather than expectation. Instead of seeking confirmation of what one wants to hear, the cards invite an open exploration of possibilities. The more you engage with them as a reflective tool, the more useful they become.

The Role of Intuition in Reading Tarot

Intuition is central to reading Tarot. The cards provide visual cues, but interpretation comes from within. Intuition is that quiet knowing that does not rely on logic or reasoning - it is the ability to sense meaning beyond the obvious.

When first learning Tarot, many rely on guidebooks or memorized meanings, but true reading happens when one allows intuition to guide the process. The best readings come when one connects with the imagery, the emotions it evokes and the personal associations it triggers. You can then refer to the guidebooks for extra clarification or for anything you may have missed.

One way to strengthen intuition is to pay attention to first impressions when drawing a card. The initial thought, feeling or image that comes to mind is often the most intuitive response. Instead of immediately reaching for a guidebook, sit with the card and notice what it sparks within you. Another effective method is to focus on the imagery itself. Each card is designed with symbols that hold meaning. Observing what details stand out, which colors or figures draw attention and how they relate to the reading can help strengthen intuitive interpretation.

Asking open-ended questions when reading also encourages intuition to lead. Instead of trying to figure out what a card means in a rigid sense, ask what message it is trying to communicate in the moment. The same card can convey different things depending on the context of the reading and the person receiving it.

A simple daily practice can also help develop intuitive reading. Drawing a card each morning and reflecting on how it connects to experiences throughout the day strengthens the connection between intuition and Tarot. Keeping a record of these daily pulls allows for those previously mentioned patterns to emerge over time, reinforcing trust in your ability to read beyond the surface. Trusting intuition takes time, especially for those who are used to relying on logic. The more one practices, the more natural it becomes.

Trusting Yourself and the Reading Process

One of the biggest challenges in reading Tarot is not learning all the card meanings, it's actually self-doubt. Many second-guess their interpretations, wondering if they are reading the cards correctly. Trust is essential - not just in the cards but in yourself.

Tarot readings are not about getting a single correct answer. Each reading is a dialogue between the reader and the cards, shaped by personal experience, intuition and perception. The same card may have different meanings in different readings because context matters.

Building confidence in reading Tarot comes from trusting the first interpretation that arises. The first thought or feeling about a card is often the most intuitive and should not be dismissed too quickly. Over-analyzing can lead to second-guessing and a loss of the natural flow of the reading. Letting go of the need to be right is also important. There is no absolute right or wrong meaning in Tarot. What matters is what resonates in the moment and what insight it provides for the person receiving the reading.

Reading without pressure allows intuition to flow more naturally. Treating Tarot as a conversation rather than a test to get the meaning right creates a more open and impactful reading experience. Revisiting past readings can also strengthen trust in the process. Sometimes, meaning becomes clearer with time. Reviewing old readings can reveal how the messages in the cards played out or how your understanding has deepened over time. Confidence comes with practice. The more you work with the cards, the more natural interpreting them becomes.

Common Misconceptions about Tarot

There are many misconceptions about Tarot, often shaped by media portrayals or misinformation. One of the most common misunderstandings is that Tarot is a fortune-telling tool that predicts a fixed future. In reality, Tarot reflects present energies and possibilities, not set outcomes. It provides guidance and insight rather than absolute answers.

Another common belief is that one must be psychic to read Tarot. This is not the case. Tarot is a system based on symbolism and intuition. Anyone can learn to read the cards with practice and an open mind. It is not about having supernatural abilities but about developing a connection with the imagery and allowing personal insights to come through.

There is also a misconception that Tarot is dangerous or invites negative energy. Tarot is simply a tool. The intention and mindset of the reader determines the experience. Just like any other tool for self-reflection, Tarot is neutral. It is how it is used that gives it meaning.

Some believe that Tarot must follow strict rules, but every reader develops their own style and approach. There is no single right way to read the cards. Some people choose to follow traditional interpretations, while others read more intuitively. Both methods are valid, and the most important thing is finding what works best for the individual.

Another outdated myth is that a Tarot deck must be gifted rather than purchased. There is no rule stating this. Many readers choose their own decks because connecting with the imagery and symbolism is important for effective readings. Finding a deck that resonates personally is far more important than where it comes from. Clearing up these misconceptions allows for a more open and simplified approach to working with the cards.

Purchasing a Deck and Looking After it

Choosing a Tarot deck is a personal decision. There are many different decks, each with unique artwork, themes and interpretations. The most important factor is finding a deck that resonates visually and energetically.

When selecting a deck, consider how the imagery feels. Some decks follow traditional Rider-Waite-Smith symbolism, while others take a more Crowley or *De Marseille* approach – don't worry I'll be covering these in the Three Traditions section. The artwork should feel engaging and meaningful, as personal connection plays a big role in reading the cards effectively. The structure of the deck is also worth considering.

While most Tarot decks follow the same seventy-eight-card format, some may have unique variations or additional cards. Looking through sample images or a guidebook can help determine if the deck aligns with you or not. Sometimes I just the box and I'm all like, "Yes please! Add to cart!", because purchasing cards should be an intuitive process.

Once a deck is chosen, taking care of it ensures it remains in good condition. Storing it in a pouch, box or wrapped in cloth helps protect the cards from wear. Also take into consideration your shuffling methods and their potential wear on your cards. It can also be helpful to be mindful of where you are reading. You'll want to avoid food and drink nearby to prevent any unwanted spills on those shiny new cards and while candles are great to burn for intention setting, its best to set that intention over a different table.

Handling the deck with intention and using it regularly builds familiarity and connection. Some readers like to cleanse their deck periodically, especially if it has been used in heavy emotional readings. This can be done by shuffling and resetting the cards back into their chronological order, placing a piece of quartz with the deck, or simply setting the intention to clear any stagnant energy. There is no strict way to store or care for a deck. What matters most is that it feels comfortable to work with and remains in good condition for long-term use.

Chapter 3

Interpreting the Tarot

Reading by Association and Intuition

As humans, we experience life through a process of association. We see reality through a lens shaped by our inner state, emotion and past experiences. This same principle applies when reading Tarot. The way one interprets the cards is influenced by personal associations, memories and perspectives. This is why no two readers interpret the same card in exactly the same way.

Interpreting the cards is an intuitive process. Reading and interpreting go hand in hand, but they are not the same. Reading Tarot is about recognizing symbols and patterns, while interpretation is the intuitive process of understanding what those symbols mean in a given context. One cannot exist without the other.

Consider The Hermit card. One reader may see this card and interpret it as a sign that the person being read for is in a period of deep introspection, seeking answers from within. Another reader may see the same card and interpret it as a sign of loneliness or emotional isolation. Both interpretations are valid, as they reflect different perspectives on the same archetype. The meaning that resonates most in a reading will be the one the person needs to hear at that moment. This is how intuition works, when something needs to be known, it will find a way to make itself clear.

At times, aspects of a reading may not make sense immediately. When this happens, it is useful to make note of the details that seem unclear and return to them later. Sometimes, new insights emerge with time. Alternatively, you can expand on a card by drawing another card for clarity. This can help provide additional perspective. Every card is pulled for a reason. Unless one is over-reading or drawing cards beyond necessity, there is always a message in what appears.

It is also worth checking in with oneself when a card seems confusing. Sometimes, the message is clear, but you may be resistant to acknowledging it. This is common, as Tarot often highlights truths that are not always comfortable to face. Learning to be honest with yourself in these moments is an important part of working with the cards.

Why Interpretations Differ from Reader to Reader

One of the most common concerns for beginners is whether they are reading Tarot "correctly." The truth is, there is no single correct way to interpret a card. Each person brings their own experiences, emotions and intuitive insights into a reading, which is why two people can pull the same card for the same question and arrive at completely different interpretations. I've seen it happen time and again over my years of teaching.

Personal perception plays a major role in how a card is read. A person who has just gone through a period of personal transformation may see the Tower as a symbol of necessary change, while someone who fears uncertainty may view it as a warning of chaos. Neither interpretation is wrong - they are simply reflections of the reader's perspective at that moment.

Because interpretation is personal, readers should trust their instincts. There is no need to memorize rigid meanings or worry about being "right." What matters is how the card speaks to you.

It is also important to recognize that Tarot is not a fixed system. Symbols hold universal meanings, but the way they are applied will always vary depending on context. A single card can hold different meanings in different readings, which is why Tarot remains a dynamic and evolving practice.

Symbolism in Tarot

Tarot is built on a foundation of symbolism. Each card is filled with imagery, colors, numbers and themes that contribute to its meaning. Understanding these symbolic elements deepens interpretation and allows for more insightful readings.

Imagery plays a significant role in Tarot. The figures, landscapes and objects depicted in the cards provide clues to their meaning. For example, the Chariot often features a figure controlling two opposing forces, symbolizing willpower and determination. A stormy sky in a card may indicate turmoil, while a calm background suggests stability. Paying attention to these details can add layers to a reading.

Colors also hold meaning. Bright yellows and golds in a card often represent enlightenment, positivity or confidence, while deep blues can symbolize intuition and inner wisdom. Red may indicate passion, action or conflict, depending on the context. Observing color patterns within a spread can reveal underlying themes in a reading.

Numbers in Tarot add another dimension to interpretation. Each number carries an energetic quality that influences the card's meaning. Aces represent new beginnings, twos indicate balance or duality, threes symbolize growth, and so on. Understanding numerology within the cards provides additional insight into their messages.

Themes run throughout the Tarot, tying the cards together into a cohesive system. The suits of the Minor Arcana each represent different aspects of life - wands correspond to action and ambition, cups to emotions and relationships, swords to intellect and communication, and pentacles to material and physical concerns. The Major Arcana follows a broader narrative of personal transformation, illustrating key lessons and experiences encountered on life's path. Recognizing these overarching themes helps create a clearer picture in a reading.

Understanding Negative Cards

A common challenge for those working with the cards is handling "negative" cards. Some cards, like the Tower, Death, or the Ten of Swords, can feel intimidating when they appear in a reading. However, labeling them as purely negative is a misunderstanding of Tarot's structure.

Tarot reflects all aspects of life - the challenges, transformations and growth that come with being human. Difficult cards do not always indicate disaster. Instead, they often highlight necessary changes, areas of resistance or opportunities for growth. Where you do find they discuss impending doom, there will always be another card accompanying them to show you how to navigate your way through.

Take the Tower, for example. While it can indicate sudden upheaval, it also represents breaking free from false foundations. The Death card is not about literal death, but transformation and endings that create space for something new. The Ten of Swords may signify rock bottom, but it also marks the beginning of building your way back up.

Rather than fearing these cards, it is important to approach them with an open mind. They often provide some of the most useful guidance, showing where change is needed and where new perspectives can be found.

Reverse Cards

Another common question in Tarot is whether to use reversed cards - cards that appear upside down in a spread. Some readers choose to work with reversals, while others do not. There is no right or wrong approach.

If reversals are used, they do not always indicate a negative meaning. Instead, they often suggest a different perspective or an internalized version of the card's energy. A reversed card may indicate delays, subconscious influences or a need for introspection.

For example, the Sun in reverse does not mean the absence of joy, but may suggest that happiness is present but not fully realized. The Eight of Wands reversed may indicate slower progress rather than total stagnation. The key is to interpret reversals in the context of the surrounding cards and the overall reading.

Readers who prefer not to use reversals can still achieve depth in their readings by considering the full spectrum of a card's meaning. Every Tarot card carries both light and shadow aspects, and awareness of this duality allows for a balanced approach to interpretation.

How to Refine Interpretations

Interpreting Tarot is a skill that develops over time. While intuition is the guiding force behind a reading, there are ways to refine interpretation to make readings more accurate and insightful.

One effective method is to focus on the overall feeling of a reading before breaking it down into individual card meanings. Rather than looking at each card separately, observe how they interact with one another. The connections between the cards often provide more clarity than any single card on its own. With that being said, there is also absolutely nothing wrong with pulling just a single card. Sometimes a single card is all you need.

Noticing patterns in a spread can also enhance interpretation. Repeating numbers, recurring suits or dominant colors may indicate an important message. Recognizing these patterns helps create a more cohesive interpretation.

Taking time to sit with a reading and allow insights to unfold naturally is another valuable approach. Tarot is not always about immediate answers. Sometimes, meanings become clearer with reflection. Revisiting readings after a few days can reveal new layers of understanding.

Expanding on difficult or unclear cards by drawing additional cards for context is another way to refine interpretation. Rather than forcing a meaning, allow the cards to build on one another. Asking specific follow-up questions can help clarify the message being conveyed.

The key to refining Tarot interpretation is trust. Trusting one's intuition, trusting the cards and trusting that the right message will come through. Interpretation is not about perfection - it is about connection.

Chapter 4

Uses for the Tarot

Tarot is a versatile tool that extends far beyond simple divination. While many people associate it with predicting the future, its value lies in its ability to deepen self-awareness, provide guidance and serve as a reflective tool for personal insight and growth. Tarot can be used in a variety of ways, from structured self-inquiry to creative inspiration, problem-solving and emotional processing. This chapter explores different ways Tarot can be integrated into daily life.

Meditation and Contemplation

A Tarot card can serve as a focal point during meditation, helping to focus the mind and cultivate presence. Meditating with Tarot involves selecting a card and allowing its imagery, colors and symbols to guide your reflections. Some people set an intention, such as gaining deeper insight into a personal challenge, while others use it as an open-ended contemplative practice.

Choose a card that resonates with you and spend a few minutes simply observing it. Focus on the details of the image and notice what thoughts, emotions or sensations arise. Avoid over-analyzing and let your intuition guide the process. Journaling about the experience afterward can help integrate any insights that emerge. This method allows the subconscious to bring forth deeper awareness, helping to process emotions, recognize patterns or gain clarity on a situation.

Tarot as a Therapeutic Tool

Tarot can be a powerful medium for self-exploration and emotional processing. It allows people to externalize thoughts and feelings, making it easier to reflect on experiences, traumas and personal struggles. While it is not a substitute for professional therapy, it can be a useful complementary practice, especially when working with deep-seated fears, anxieties or life transitions.

Because Tarot is archetypal in nature, it speaks to the universal themes and inner narratives that shape human experiences. Many people find that certain cards mirror their emotions or offer a new perspective on personal challenges.

Tarot can help you with:

- Identifying limiting beliefs or behavioral patterns
- Gaining clarity on personal struggles
- Processing emotions in a non-linear, intuitive way
- Exploring one's spiritual or existential questions

When working with Tarot in this way, it is important to approach it gently and with an open mind. It can be used alongside journaling or reflection exercises to deepen self-inquiry.

Problem Solving and Decision Making

Tarot can help break through mental blocks by offering fresh perspectives on problems and challenges. It does not provide direct answers, but encourages consideration of different options and possible outcomes.

To use Tarot for problem-solving, focus on a specific issue and ask open-ended questions such as:

- What am I not seeing about this situation?
- What are my options moving forward?
- What should I be aware of before making a decision?

The cards can reveal underlying influences, potential roadblocks or new ways to approach the situation. By reflecting on their meaning, one can make more informed and conscious choices.

Self-Expression and Creativity

Sometimes it can be difficult to articulate emotions, thoughts or ideas. Tarot can serve as a visual and symbolic aid in self-expression, helping people put words to what they are feeling or experiencing.

Tarot can also act as a creative trigger, inspiring storytelling, poetry, painting or other artistic pursuits. Many writers and artists use Tarot as a source of inspiration, allowing the imagery and symbolism to spark ideas and expand creative thinking.

Journaling and Personal Reflection

Keeping a Tarot journal is one of the most effective ways to track progress and deepen understanding of the cards. Writing about readings can provide valuable insight over time, revealing recurring themes, personal growth and shifting perspectives.

A Tarot journal can be used to:

- Record daily card pulls and reflections
- Track patterns in readings over time
- Explore personal interpretations of different cards
- Work through emotions and thoughts more clearly

Journaling does not need to be structured or formal. Simply writing down thoughts, impressions and connections to life experiences can enhance both intuitive and intellectual engagement with the cards.

Soul Work and Personal Growth

Tarot can be used to explore deeper aspects of the self, helping to uncover truths that may not be immediately apparent. It aligns well with soul work, where the goal is to gain insight into personal growth, transformation and life purpose.

This type of work often involves looking at recurring life themes, strengths and challenges. The major arcana can be particularly useful here, as the cards represent different stages of growth and development.

Seeking Guidance without Dependency

Tarot is often sought for guidance, but it is important to use it as a tool rather than a crutch. The cards should not be relied on for making decisions, but instead used to gain perspective and clarity.

Guidance-based Tarot readings can help with:

- Understanding where one stands in a situation
- Identifying opportunities or challenges
- Exploring possible directions without forcing a specific outcome

A balanced approach ensures that Tarot remains an empowering tool rather than something that dictates choices.

Introspection and Shadow Work

Introspection involves using Tarot to explore inner thoughts, motivations and emotional patterns. This can be particularly helpful in uncovering unconscious beliefs and behaviors that shape actions and decisions.

Shadow work is a deeper form of introspection where one acknowledges and works with hidden or suppressed aspects of the self. Tarot can be used to identify areas for growth and healing by bringing these aspects to light in a nonjudgmental way.

Questions for introspective and shadow work include:

- What parts of myself am I not acknowledging?
- What patterns do I keep repeating?
- What can I learn from this challenge?

Tarot can help with processing these insights, allowing for greater self-acceptance and transformation.

Developing Intuition

Working with Tarot naturally strengthens intuition. The more one engages with the cards, the easier it becomes to trust inner knowing and instinctual responses.

Practicing intuitive Tarot can involve:

- Pulling a daily card and reflecting on its relevance throughout the day
- Reading without a guidebook, relying on personal interpretation
- Using free association with card imagery instead of memorized meanings

Over time, this practice can enhance confidence in reading the cards and deepen overall intuitive awareness.

Tarot is not limited to a single use or approach. It is a flexible tool that can be adapted to suit different needs, whether for spiritual exploration, emotional processing, creativity or decision-making. Learning to integrate Tarot into daily life can make it a valuable companion for self-awareness, insight and transformation.

Chapter 5

Questioning the Tarot

The Importance of Asking the Right Questions

Tarot is a tool for insight, guidance, and self-awareness, but the quality of the answers you receive depends on the questions you ask. Formulating the right questions ensures that your readings are meaningful, empowering, and provide clarity rather than confusion.

Before drawing cards, it is helpful to be clear on why you are consulting Tarot. Are you seeking guidance on a decision, clarity on a situation, or deeper self-awareness? The more precise your intention, the more valuable your reading will be.

A common mistake is asking the cards for definitive answers or fixed predictions. While Tarot can highlight patterns, possibilities, and potential outcomes, it does not dictate a single unchangeable future. The cards reflect energy, personal choices, and influencing factors, but they do not remove responsibility from the person asking the question.

Instead of asking, "will I get the job?", a more effective question would be, "what can I do to improve my chances of getting the job?" or, "what should I be aware of regarding this opportunity?" This shifts the focus from passive waiting to active engagement with the situation.

Framing Effective and Insightful Questions

Effective Tarot questions are:

- Open-ended rather than yes or no
- Empowering rather than dependent
- Focused on the present and near future
- Insight-driven rather than predictive
- Clear and specific rather than vague or overly detailed

When phrasing a question, consider what type of guidance you are seeking. A question like, "what energy surrounds this situation?" offers insight into the current state of things, while, "what steps can I take to move forward?" provides actionable direction.

Examples of strong questions:

- What should I be aware of in this situation?
- What strengths can I lean on right now?
- What is blocking me from moving forward?
- How can I navigate this challenge?
- What perspective am I not seeing?

Types of Questions Can and Cannot Be Asked
Questions That Can Be Asked

- Self-awareness and personal growth. How can I deepen my self-understanding?
- Spiritual exploration. What aspects of my spiritual path should I focus on?
- Clarification on situations. What do I need to understand about this relationship?
- Guidance on decisions. What should I consider before making this choice?
- Emotional processing. What is at the root of this feeling?

Questions That Should Be Avoided

- Fixed predictions. Will I get married next year?
- Removing personal responsibility. What should I do?
- Gambling or chance-based inquiries. What are the lottery numbers?
- Invasive questions about others. How does my ex feel about me?
- Unethical questions. Will someone else fail at their job?
- Yes or no questions. Will I be successful? Instead, ask: What steps can I take to ensure success?

Sample Questions:
How can I make better progress on my path?

Wheel of Fortune

- Deck: Ethereal Visions Tarot, Matt Hughes
- Cards: Major Arcana
- Card Drawn: Wheel of Fortune

When looking at how one could make better progress, the Wheel of Fortune is an instant indicator that change is the solution. The Wheel represents cycles, shifts, and movement. To progress, embracing change is necessary. Resisting it may cause stagnation. By aligning with life's natural ebb and flow, progress becomes smoother and more intentional.

What aspects of my personality could I improve?

Queen of Swords

- Deck: Gothic Tarot, Anne Stokes
- Cards: Court Cards
- Card Drawn: Queen of Swords

The Queen of Swords highlights the importance of mental clarity, self-assurance, and logical thinking. This suggests a need to develop strong boundaries, approach situations with intelligence rather than emotion, and communicate clearly. However, it also warns against becoming too detached or cutting off emotions entirely.

What aspect of myself should I focus on?

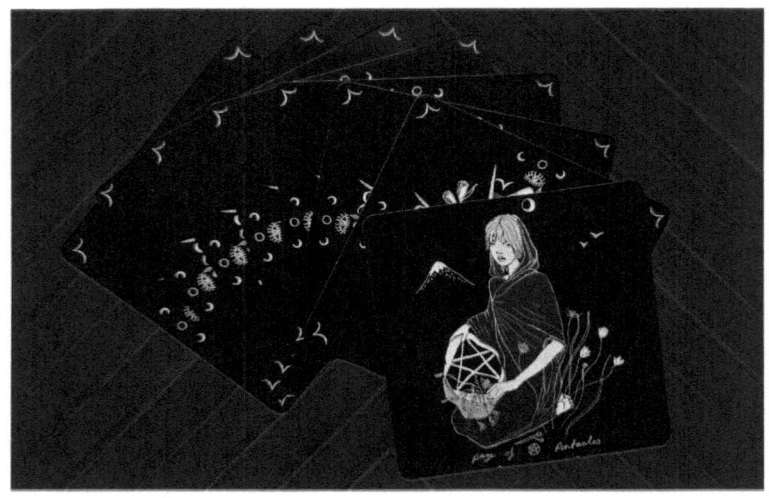

Page of Pentacles

- Deck: Dark Days Tarot, Emily Mundy & Wren McMurdo
- Cards: Court Cards
- Card Drawn: Page of Pentacles

The Page of Pentacles encourages a focus on learning, growth and practical skills. This card suggests that it is time to commit to developing a new skill or refining existing ones. Whether this relates to career, health or personal development, the emphasis is on steady progress, patience and dedication to long-term improvement.

What am I not seeing in my current situation?

The Magus

- Deck: Tarot of the Spirit, Pamela Eakins & Joyce Eakins
- Cards: Major Arcana
- Card Drawn: The Magus

The Magus represents potential, personal power, and the ability to manifest change. If this card appears in response to what is being overlooked, it suggests that one may not be fully recognizing their own skills, talents, or ability to take control of their circumstances. There may be untapped potential waiting to be explored, or an opportunity that is being dismissed due to self-doubt or hesitation.

What is influencing my current choices?

Seven of Cups

- Deck: Gilded Tarot, Ciro Marchetti
- Cards: Minor Arcana
- Card Drawn: Seven of Cups

The Seven of Cups points to confusion, distractions or an overwhelming number of choices. This suggests that external influences or internal uncertainty are clouding decision-making. It may be beneficial to focus on priorities, clear away illusions and be mindful of where energy is being directed. Not all options presented may be realistic or beneficial and careful discernment is needed.

Chapter 6

Understanding Spreads

Tarot spreads provide a structured way to organize cards during a reading, offering clarity, depth and insight. A spread determines how many cards are used, their positions and what each position represents. While single-card pulls can be useful for quick insights, structured spreads allow for more detailed exploration of a question, challenge or situation.

Selecting the right spread depends on the type of reading being done. Some spreads are simple and versatile, while others are more complex and best suited for in-depth analysis. This chapter explores different types of spreads, provides sample readings, and offers guidance on creating custom spreads tailored to specific needs.

Working with Spreads

Using a spread helps to create a narrative with the cards, allowing them to interact with each other rather than being interpreted in isolation. The relationships between the cards, their positions and the flow of the reading can reveal nuances that a single-card draw might miss.

Each card in a spread does not exist in isolation. The meaning of any given card can shift depending on its surrounding cards, its placement in the spread and the question being asked.

- **Flow of the Spread:** Spreads often have a natural flow, such as past to present to future or obstacles to solutions. Recognizing this flow helps make sense of how the cards connect.
- **Card Reinforcement:** When multiple cards share a similar theme (e.g., many swords in a reading about decision-making), it strengthens the emphasis of that theme.
- **Contrasting Messages:** Sometimes, a reading includes seemingly opposing cards, such as the Fool and the Emperor. This contrast highlights inner conflicts, dual perspectives, or choices that need balance.
- **Card Progressions:** Certain spreads allow for movement within a reading, showing growth, setbacks or necessary shifts. For example, the Five of Pentacles followed by the Six of Pentacles could indicate a transition from financial struggle to support or balance.
- **Major vs. Minor Arcana:** If a spread has multiple major arcana cards, it suggests larger, more transformative life events. A spread dominated by minor arcana indicates day-to-day matters and influences.

Understanding these connections makes readings more insightful and layered. With practice, it becomes easier to see how cards influence each other within the spread.

Choosing the Right Spread

Before beginning a reading, it is essential to define the theme or question. The spread should complement the intention behind the reading. Do be weary of information overload, however, as it can sometimes be tempting to just draw one more. If you see repeated information coming through that is a good indicate that there is nothing more to be said about the matter. In some places in life, size does matter, so when choosing your spread look at the number of cards being used and what all those cards are pointing to.

- **Small spreads** (one to five cards) are useful for quick guidance, daily reflections and focused questions.
- **Larger spreads** (six or more cards) provide deeper insights into layered or complex situations, relationships and long-term patterns.

There is no single right or wrong way to use spreads. Some readers prefer traditional or pre-created layouts, while others create their own. The key is finding what works best for the reading at hand.

Creating Your Own Spread

Existing spreads offer a wealth of insights, creating a personal spread, however, allows for a more tailored reading. A custom spread should reflect the specific nature of the question or situation being explored.

To create a spread:

1. Define the purpose of the reading. What is being asked or examined?
2. Determine the number of cards needed. A simple question may require only three to five cards, while a complex situation might need more.
3. Assign meaning to each card position. For example, a three-card spread might represent past, present and future, while a five-card spread could focus on strengths, weaknesses, external influences, challenges and advice.
4. Lay out the cards in a way that makes sense for the question. Linear, circular, or pyramid-like formations are all possible. Let your imagination run wild!
5. Experimenting with different layouts can help refine a spread that works best.

Sample Spreads

Below are some commonly known spreads along with some I've created for this guidebook specifically to help illustrate their application.

Simple Three-Card Timeline Spread

Simple Three-Card Timeline Spread

Question: What do I need to focus on right now?
Deck Used: Modern Witch Tarot

1. **What Have I Been Focusing On? – Five of Cups**
   A recent disappointment or emotional setback has left lingering feelings of regret or sadness. This card suggests a focus on what has been lost rather than recognizing what remains. There may be unresolved grief or unprocessed emotions that are weighing heavily, preventing forward movement. While the pain is valid, the Five of Cups also encourages a shift in perspective - what lessons can be taken from this situation?
2. **What Should I Be Focusing On? – The Fool**
   A new beginning is unfolding, offering an opportunity to step into the unknown with openness and curiosity. The Fool represents a fresh start, but only if one is willing to take the leap and embrace the moment without fear. This card calls for trust in the process, encouraging a sense of playfulness and spontaneity rather than being held back by past regrets.
3. **Where Could My New Focus Potentially Lead? – The Sun**
   Positive potential outcomes are ahead, bringing clarity, joy and renewed energy. The Sun reassures that after hardship, things will begin to align in a more fulfilling way. Should one be able to shift their focus as needed, optimism, confidence and happiness become more accessible.

This reading suggests that the focus should be on shifting perspective from past disappointments to new opportunities. The Fool and the Sun together reinforce a theme of embracing change and trusting that joy and success are attainable when old wounds are no longer the dominant focus.

Growth Like Trees Spread

Growth Like Trees Spread

Question: How can I improve my personal growth?
Deck Used: Wild Unknown Tarot

1. **Where Am I Currently Rooted? — The Hermit**
   The Hermit signals a time of introspection and self-exploration. There may be a need for solitude to reflect

on past experiences and inner wisdom. This card suggests that personal growth is best nurtured through self-awareness and time spent understanding one's deeper motivations.

2. **What has me Root-Bound? — Eight of Swords**
   A feeling of being trapped, whether by limiting beliefs or external circumstances, is preventing progress. The Eight of Swords highlights mental barriers - fears, self-doubt or restrictive thought patterns. The challenge lies in recognizing that these constraints are self-imposed and can be removed through awareness and action.

3. **How to Sprout — Knight of Wands**
   The Knight of Wands urges bold action and enthusiasm. This card suggests that instead of overthinking or hesitating, it is important to move forward with confidence. Passion and energy are available to fuel personal development, but action must be taken without fear of making mistakes.

4. **Current Weather Conditions (External Influences) — Ace of Pentacles**
   A new opportunity or resource may present itself in the physical realm—this could be a job opportunity, a course of study or a chance to invest in oneself in a tangible way. The Ace of Pentacles encourages recognizing and seizing these opportunities to support long-term growth.

5. **Possible Direction of Growth — The World**
   If the advice is followed, a sense of completion and fulfillment awaits. The World represents personal

achievement, self-realization and an integration of past lessons into newfound wisdom. It signifies arriving at a place of inner harmony and clarity.

This spread suggests that personal growth is hindered by self-imposed limitations, but with introspection (The Hermit) and bold action (Knight of Wands), these barriers can be overcome. Opportunities for tangible progress (Ace of Pentacles) should be embraced, as they lead to deep fulfillment (The World).

The Celtic Cross Spread

The Celtic Cross Spread

Question: What perspective should be considered in shifting toward a career with more meaning?
Deck Used: Light Seer's Tarot

1. **Current Position — Six of Pentacles**
There is a desire for balance between giving and receiv-

ing. Opportunities exist to engage in meaningful work, particularly in areas of service or support. However, it is important to ensure that generosity is not leading to depletion.

2. **Immediate Influence – Five of Cups**
   Past disappointments and failures may be casting doubt on the ability to succeed in a new career direction. The fear of repeating mistakes or facing loss again could be preventing forward movement.

3. **Recent Past – Seven of Cups**
   A period of indecision has led to questioning current career paths. There may have been many options available, creating confusion about the right direction.

4. **Immediate Future – Page of Wands**
   If action is taken, progress can unfold quickly. This card suggests an opportunity to explore new directions with enthusiasm and curiosity.

5. **Hopes and Desires – Eight of Wands**
   A strong desire for rapid change and movement is present. The need for a shift is pressing, and there is excitement around stepping into something new.

6. **Immediate Thoughts – Queen of Cups**
   The decision-making process is being guided by deep emotional awareness and intuition. There is a pull toward work that aligns with inner values and emotional fulfillment.

7. **External Influence – Nine of Wands**
   Old commitments or unfinished business may need to be resolved before fully embracing a new path. There

may be resistance from external sources or a lingering sense of responsibility toward a past role.
8. **Your Influence – The Tower**
Transformation is necessary for true change. Holding onto old structures will not lead to fulfillment. The Tower signals that a major shift must happen to clear the way for something new.
9. **Hopes and Fears – Page of Pentacles**
Success is both desired and feared. There is excitement about starting fresh, but also concern about whether it will lead to tangible success.
10. **Potential Outcome – Seven of Pentacles**
Achievements are possible, but they require patience and long-term investment. Success will not be immediate, but sustained effort will yield positive results. This reading highlights the need to release past disappointments (Five of Cups) and take action toward change (Page of Wands). While external factors (Nine of Wands) may create obstacles, deep transformation (The Tower) is necessary for fulfillment. The outcome (Seven of Pentacles) suggests that rewards will come with time and dedication.

The Raven Spread

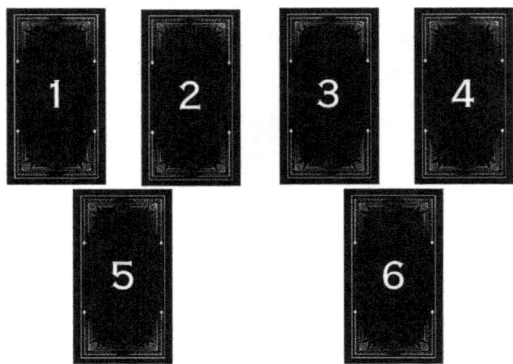

The Raven Spread

Question: Should I stay where I am, or is it time to move on?
Deck Used: New Era Elements Tarot

1. **What You Are — Ten of Cups**
   There is a sense of comfort and familiarity, but it may be masking complacency. Things feel stable, but true fulfillment is lacking.
2. **What You Could Be — The Devil**
   Facing fears and breaking free from stagnation is needed. There may be subconscious attachments to routine or security that are preventing progress.
3. **What is Currently Happening — Ace of Swords**
   Clarity is emerging, making it easier to see the reality of the situation. There may be an internal awakening or realization that change is necessary.
4. **Potential Events — Six of Swords**
   A transition is likely, whether it is chosen or happens naturally. Moving into a new phase will bring relief and a sense of forward movement.
5. **What to Avoid — Eight of Cups**
   Walking away too soon without fully understanding the situation could lead to regret. Ensure that all angles have been explored before making a final decision.
6. **What to Look for — The High Priestess**
   Trust in intuition is key. The answers are already known deep within, and taking time for reflection will provide clarity.

This reading suggests that comfort (Ten of Cups) may be preventing deeper fulfillment. While fears (The Devil) need to be addressed, a transition (Six of Swords) is likely. However, it is important not to rush the decision (Eight of Cups). The High Priestess advises trusting intuition when determining the right path.

The Pyramid Spread

The Pyramid Spread

Question: Where is my energy going and why am I feeling exhausted?
Deck Used: Morgan Greer Tarot

1. **The Question – Strength**

Energy depletion is a core concern and Strength indicates that much of this exhaustion comes from constantly exerting control, patience and perseverance. There may be a sense of having to remain strong for others, constantly pushing forward without taking time for personal restoration. This card signals the need to assess where energy is being spent and whether it is sustainable.

2. **Root of the Matter – The Magician**
   Power is present but may not be used effectively. The Magician suggests that skills, resources and personal willpower are being scattered or misapplied. Instead of focusing on aligned action, energy may be diverted into obligations or responsibilities that are not serving personal well-being. The key here is to realign focus, recognizing that having the ability to do something does not mean it must always be done.

3. **Mind's Perspective – Wheel of Fortune**
   Mentally, there is an awareness that change is necessary. The Wheel of Fortune represents cycles, and in this context, it suggests a pattern of overexertion followed by burnout. This card encourages shifting perspective, recognizing that exhaustion is not a fixed state but something that can be adjusted through conscious decisions. Learning to work with energy cycles rather than against them is crucial.

4. **Heart's Perspective – Queen of Cups**
   Emotionally, there is a deep need for self-care. The Queen of Cups is a nurturing figure, but in this position, she highlights the importance of turning that care inward rather than constantly giving to others.

The heart is calling for emotional restoration, time for reflection, and perhaps even setting boundaries to prevent further depletion.
5. **Sacrifices — Ten of Wands**
The burden of carrying too much must be released. The Ten of Wands is a card of overburdening, taking on responsibilities that should be shared or let go. There may be obligations that have been assumed out of duty, but this card urges a reassessment of what truly needs to be carried versus what has been unnecessarily taken on.
6. **Challenges — Six of Pentacles**
Over-giving is a major contributing factor to exhaustion. This card suggests an imbalance in energy exchange - perhaps more is being given than received. Whether this applies to work, relationships or personal obligations, the key challenge is to find a way to give in a way that does not lead to depletion.
7. **Unexpected Factors — King of Cups**
Emotional balance is key, and it may come in an unexpected way. The King of Cups represents mastery over emotions and suggests that stability can be achieved through emotional intelligence and control. There may be a need to step back from reacting emotionally to every demand and instead approach situations from a place of calm and measured response.
8. **Positive Influences — The World**
A shift in perspective will open new doors. The World is a card of completion and fulfillment, suggesting that a healthier approach to energy management will lead

to greater satisfaction in all areas of life. Taking the necessary steps to create balance will not only prevent burnout but will also allow for a more harmonious existence.

9. **Suggested Outcome – Five of Wands**
   Awareness of energy placement is crucial. The Five of Wands often signifies scattered energy and conflict, which in this case, suggests that a lack of clear boundaries or direction has contributed to exhaustion. The suggested course of action is to assess where energy is going and make intentional adjustments to prevent unnecessary struggles.

10. **Potential Outcome – Two of Cups**
    Achieving balance through self-prioritization is the ultimate outcome. The Two of Cups is a card of harmony, mutual respect and balance. If conscious effort is made to manage energy wisely, relationships, work and personal well-being will improve, leading to a state of greater fulfillment and peace.

This reading highlights the need to redistribute energy and avoid burnout by recognizing where energy is being drained unnecessarily. Strength and the Magician indicate that power and endurance are present, but they are being misdirected. The Wheel of Fortune suggests that cycles of exhaustion can be broken and the Queen of Cups and King of Cups reinforce the importance of emotional self-care. Letting go of unnecessary burdens (Ten of Wands) and addressing over-giving (Six of Pentacles) will open the door to a more sustainable way of living. The ultimate message is to become more intentional with energy use, allowing for true balance and fulfillment.

Chapter 7

The Three Traditions

Before exploring the cards in depth, understanding the three main Tarot traditions can provide useful context. While this guidebook is structured around the Smith-Waite system, elements of the Thoth tradition are also incorporated, and aspects of the simplicity found in the Tarot de Marseille influence how the Minor Arcana is presented. This section offers an overview of these traditions, making it easier to cross-reference between them and gain insight into their unique structures and approaches.

Tarot De Marseille

The Tarot de Marseille is one of the oldest surviving Tarot traditions and serves as the foundation for both the Smith-Waite and Thoth systems. It remains popular in French-speaking countries and is still used for its original purpose as a card game. The most distinct characteristic of this deck is the structure of its Minor Arcana, which closely resembles a deck of playing cards.

Instead of detailed illustrations depicting scenes, the numbered cards - referred to as Pips - simply show a symbolic representation of their number and suit.

For example, the Five of Cups in a *De Marseille* deck will display five cups arranged in a pattern, without additional imagery to suggest interpretation. This style requires the reader to apply meanings based on number and suit associations rather than relying on visual storytelling. While this can seem challenging, it also allows for a more open reading experience, free from subconscious influence by imagery.

In the *De Marseille* system, the Minor Arcana follows a structured meaning across suits. All Aces share a similar function but express themselves differently based on suit - such as the Ace of Wands representing a new creative endeavor, while the Ace of Pentacles signals new material opportunities. The Major Arcana, on the other hand, follows the same archetypal journey as other traditions, making it easy to apply interpretations across different decks.

Smith-Waite

The Smith-Waite tradition, also called the Rider-Waite-Smith, is the most widely recognized and used in English-speaking countries. Created by Arthur Edward Waite and illustrated by Pamela Colman Smith in 1909, this was the first deck designed specifically for esoteric study. Waite and Smith were members of the Hermetic Order of the Golden Dawn, a metaphysical society that incorporated Tarot into its teachings, though Waite's goal was to make Tarot accessible to the general public rather than limiting it to initiates of secret orders. The defining feature of this tradition is its fully illustrated Minor Arcana. Unlike the *De Marseille* tradition, each card in the Smith-Waite deck contains a detailed scene, giving the reader visual prompts that make intuitive interpretation easier. This makes it an ideal starting point for those new to Tarot, as the storytelling aspect of the imagery allows for a more natural connection to the meanings.

While the Smith-Waite system retains some Kabbalistic and astrological influences, these are more subtle than in the Thoth deck, making it a more approachable system for general use. Many modern Tarot decks are based on this structure, following the same card order, naming conventions, and imagery style, making it the most widely recognized and universally applicable tradition.

Crowley, Thoth

The Thoth Tarot, created by Aleister Crowley and illustrated by Lady Frieda Harris, was developed over five years but was not published until 1969, after both creators had passed. Crowley was a highly controversial mystic and the founder of Thelema, a spiritual philosophy based on esoteric teachings. Unlike the Smith-Waite deck, the Thoth Tarot is deeply embedded with alchemical, astrological and Kabbalistic symbolism, making it a complex but powerful system for those drawn to deeper occult traditions.

The Minor Arcana in the Thoth deck differs from both the *De Marseille* and Smith-Waite systems. While it does not feature full pictorial scenes like the Smith-Waite deck, it is not as minimalist as the *De Marseille* Pips. Instead, each card is infused with intricate symbolism that requires knowledge of astrological and Hermetic correspondences. For this reason, working with the Thoth Tarot often requires study beyond the guidebook, particularly in areas such as Kabbalah, alchemy and ceremonial magic.

Readers who are familiar with these subjects often find the Thoth Tarot to be one of the most intellectually and spiritually rich decks available. The structure of the deck aligns more closely with Hermetic initiation paths, making it an ideal choice for those working within esoteric traditions. However, for those without a background in these teachings, the dense symbolism can present a steep learning curve.

Cross-Referencing Between Traditions

When choosing a deck, it is important to find a system that resonates personally. Those who prefer a straightforward, structured approach may gravitate toward the *De Marseille* tradition, while those who seek rich visual storytelling often find the Smith-Waite deck most accessible. For those drawn to deeper esoteric study, the Thoth deck provides an advanced framework filled with layered symbolism.

For readers working with multiple traditions, it is helpful to understand how meanings translate between them. The Major Arcana remains largely consistent across all three traditions, though naming and ordering may vary slightly. The Minor Arcana, however, differs in its presentation - ranging from the simplified Pips of the *De Marseille* to the fully illustrated Smith-Waite and the symbol-heavy Thoth system. Understanding these differences can make it easier to transition between decks and apply knowledge across different traditions.

If unsure about which tradition a deck belongs to, checking the guidebook or researching the deck's origins can help clarify its structure. The reference sheets following this section will highlight key differences between traditions, along with base meanings drawn from traditional interpretations and personal insights.

SMITH-WAITE	THOTH	DE MARSEILLE
SUIT NAMES		
PENTACLES	DISKS	COINS
WANDS	WANDS	BATONS/STAVES
CUPS	CUPS	CUPS
SWORDS	SWORDS	SWORDS
COURT NAMES		
PAGES	PRINCESS	KNAVE
KNIGHT	PRINCE	KNIGHT
QUEEN	QUEEN	QUEEN
KING	KNIGHT	KING
MAJOR ARCANA NAMES | ORDERING		
THE FOOL	THE FOOL	LE MAT/THE FOOL
THE MAGICIAN	THE MAGUS	LE BATELEUR/JUGGLER
THE HIGH PRIESTESS	THE PRIESTESS	LA PAPESSE/POPESS
THE EMPRESS	THE EMPRESS	L'IMPERATRICE/EMPRESS
THE EMPEROR	THE EMPEROR	L'EMPEREUR/EMPEROR
THE HIEROPHANT	THE HIEROPHANT	LE PAPE/POPE
THE LOVERS	THE LOVERS	L'AMOUREU /LOVERS
THE CHARIOT	THE CHARIOT	LE CHARIOT/CHARIOT
STRENGTH	ADJUSTMENT	LA FORCE/STRENGTH
THE HERMIT	THE HERMIT	L'ERMITE/HERMIT
WHEEL OF FORTUNE	FORTUNE	LA ROUE / THE WHEEL
JUSTICE	LUST	LA JUSTICE /JUSTICE
THE HANGED MAN	THE HANGED MAN	LE PENDU/HANGED MAN
DEATH	DEATH	LE MORT/DEATH
TEMPERANCE	ART	TEMPÉRANCE/TEMPERANCE
THE DEVIL	THE DEVIL	LE DIABLE/DEVIL
THE TOWER	THE TOWER	LA TOUR/THE TOWER
THE STAR	THE STAR	L'ÉTOILE/THE STARS
THE MOON	THE MOON	LA LUNE/MOON
THE SUN	THE SUN	LE SOLEIL/SUN
JUDGEMENT	THE AEON	LE JUGEMENT/JUDGEMENT
THE WORLD	THE UNIVERSE	LE MONDE/WORLD

TAROT DE MARSEILLE – PIPS

THE SUITS

COINS	STAVES	CUPS	SWORDS
OBTAINING	CREATING	INTERACTING	DEFENDING
PROVIDING FOR SELF	CREATIVE ENERGY	EMOTIONS	SELF DEFENCE
TAKING RESOURFUL RISKS	INNOVATION	RELATIONSHIPS	SETTING BOUNDARIES
CREATING A COMFORT ZONE	BUILDING ENERGY	DEALINGS WITH OTHERS	MAKING YOUR MARK

NUMBERS

ACES
BEGINNINGS
SEED STAGE
FIRST TIME ROUND
TRYING NEW THINGS
OPPORTUNITY

SIXES
KEEP IT GOING
PROGRESS
MOMENTUM
OPPORTUNITY TO GIVE
HANDING THINGS OVER

TWOS
DIALOUGE
TWO PARTS
BALANCE
DUALITY
DIFFERENT OPTIONS

SEVENS
DIGGING DEEPER
DEEPER AWARENESS
HIDDEN MOTIVATIONS
NOTHING SUPERFICIAL
REALISM

THREES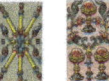
HAVING A PLAN
STRATEGY
WORKING ON A GOAL
SETTING GOALS
PREPARATION

EIGHTS
EFFECIENCY
BECOMING MASTER
DISCPLINED
STRUCTURED
SKILLED EXPERT

FOURS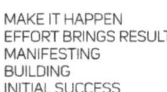
MAKE IT HAPPEN
EFFORT BRINGS RESULT
MANIFESTING
BUILDING
INITIAL SUCCESS

NINES
DESERVANCE
REWARDS
REAPING BENEFITS
REWARD FOR EFFORT
RECEIVING PROFITS

FIVES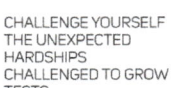
CHALLENGE YOURSELF
THE UNEXPECTED
HARDSHIPS
CHALLENGED TO GROW
TESTS

TENS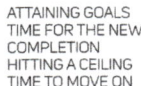
ATTAINING GOALS
TIME FOR THE NEW
COMPLETION
HITTING A CEILING
TIME TO MOVE ON

TAROT DE MARSEILLE – COURT CARDS

PAGES
LEARNING
CURIOSITY
GAINING INTEREST
SOMETHING NEW
NEW PROJECTS

QUEENS
ENCOURAGING
FEELING OF EASE
ACHIEVING WITH CALM
PERSUASION
GENTLE APPROACH

KNIGHTS
FOCUSSED
SINGLE MINDED
DETERMINATION
ENERGETIC
PROGRESSION

KINGS
CONTROLLING
USING FORCE
AUTHORITY
IMPOSING ON OTHERS
DOMINEERING

TAROT DE MARSEILLE – MAJOR ARCANA

THE FOOL

FOOLISHNESS
NONCOMFORMITY
DEVOUT
ENEXPECTED THINGS
GOOD ADVICE

THE MAGICIAN

TRICKSTER
TAKING ADVANTAGE
BEING TRICKED
OUT OF THE NORM
BEATING THE SYSTEM

HIGH POPESS

RELIGIOUS INSTITUTION
CUSTOMS
WRITTEN HISTORY
FEMININITY
OPPOSED PATRIACHY

THE EMPRESS

IDEALIZED FEMININE
ONES HOME
ROOTS
CULTURE
NUTURING

THE EMPEROR

MATERIAL POWER
SAFETY
AUTHORITY
MIGHTY CAN FALL
KNOW YOUR POWER

THE POPE

SPIRITUAL WISDOM
SPIRITUAL AUTHORITY
PETITION FOR HELP
DESERVING OF RESPECT
BE AWARE

THE LOVERS

ATTRACTION
COMPLICATIONS
NON-RATIONAL CHOICE
SENSUAL MOTIVES
COMMITMENTS

THE CHARIOT

VICTORY
HEROISM
THE RIGHT CHOICES
KNOWING
CONFIDENCE

JUSTICE

FAIRNESS
IMPARTIALITY
JUDICIAL SYSTEMS
BEING JUDGED
JUDGING OTHERS

THE HERMIT

SOLITUDE
SEARCH FOR SPIRIT
NON-RELIGIOUS
SPIRITUAL
SEARCH FOR VIRTUE

THE WHEEL

HELPLESS TO FATE
ACCEPTING LIMITS
AWARENESS OF CYCLES
FOOLISH CHOICES
PROMISE OF REBIRTH

STRENGTH

INNER STRENGTH
FORTITUDE
RESOLUTION
AVOID DISTRACTIONS
CENTRED / FOCUSSED

THE HANGED MAN

BETRAYAL
UNETHICAL
ACCUSATIONS MADE
BEING AN EXAMPLE
EMBARRESSMENT

DEATH

NEEDED ENDING
CHANGE DIRECTION
CHALLENGE VIEWS
INEVITABILITY
NATURE FORCES

TEMPERENCE

BALANCED CHARACTER
HEALTHY PSYCHE
BEING TEMPERATE
TEMPERING BEHAVIOUR
MODERATION

THE DEVIL

UNEXPECTED
CHALLENGES
TEMPTATIONS
MATERIALISM
GREED

THE TOWER

ABRUPT ENDINGS
FREEING ONESELF
REMOVING CHAINS
NO NEED FOR GLORY
SUDDEN CHANGE

THE STARS

SEARCH FOR TRUTH
HINT OF BIGGER TRUTHS
RECONCILE OPPOSITES
MERGING ONESELF
DISCOVERY

THE MOON

PERCEPTION OF TRUTH
DEEPER INSIGHTS
BROADER PERSPECTIVE
MYSTERIES
UNEASE

THE SUN

WELL-BEING
SECURITY
INNOCENCE
PEACE
CLEAR PERCEPTION

JUDGMENT

FINAL DECISIONS
JUDGING
BEING JUDGED
REALIZATIONS
REVELATIONS

THE WORLD

CONNECTION OF EVERYTHING
DIRECT EXPERIENCES
FEELING CONNECTION
SACREDNESS OF LIFE
FINDING PERMANENCE

THE ART OF TAROT GUIDEBOOK ~ 69

RIDER-SMITH – LESSER ARCANA

PENTACLES	WANDS	CUPS	SWORDS
ACES			
STABILITY / OPPORTUNITIES / ABUNDANCE / IMPROVEMENTS / ACHIEVEMENTS	NEW ENERGY / CREATIVITY / INSPIRATION / CONFIDENCE / INVENTIVENESS	NEW RELATIONSHIPS / EMPATHY / INTIMACY / INTUITION / EXPRESSING LOVE	NEW IDEAS / BEING OBJECTIVE / UNDERSTANDING / APPLY LOGIC / NEW MINDSET
TWOS			
BALANCE / COPING SKILLS / FLEXIBILITY / ADAPTABILITY / CONFIDENCE	SELF DISCIPLINE / PERSONAL POWER / SEIZE THE DAY / FACING FEARS / PIONEERING	PARTNERSHIPS / UNIONS / MUTUAL AGREEMENTS / ATTRACTION / RELATIONSHIP HEALTH	REFUSING TO ACT / BLINDED BY FEARS / AFRAID TO ACT / HIDING DISTRESS / STUCK IN A RUT
THREES			
TEAM WORK / COORDINATING / PLANNING / STRATEGY / RESOURCES	NEW PERSPECTIVE / ANTICIPATION / TAKE CHARGE / EXPAND HORIZONS / LEADERSHIP	 CELEBRATION / HIGH SPIRITS / FRIENDSHIPS / ENJOYING LIFE / UNITY WITH OTHERS	BETRAYAL / SORROW / DISAPPOINTMENT / FEELING ALONE / BROKEN TRUST
FOURS			
LETTING GO / DEMANDING / SELFISHNESS / BOUNDARIES / STUBBORN	COMPLETION / REWARDS / GOOD NEWS / ACCOMPLISHMENT / BREAKING FREE	LOST OPPORTUNITIES / APATHY / BOREDOM / DISCONNET / SELF ABSORBED	REST THE MIND / TAKE A BREAK / TAKE IT EASY / CONTEMPLATION / GAINING STABILITY
FIVES			
HARDSHIPS / LOSS / POOR HEALTH / REJECTION / INSTABILITY	MISPLACED ENERGY / PETTY QUARRELS / MINOR SETBACKS / DISAGREEMENTS / TRIVIAL PROBLEMS	SUFFERING LOSS / GRIEVING / OVERWHELMED / REGRETS / DISSAPPOINTMENT	LOSS OF MORALS / DISHONOUR / SELFISHNESS / POWER STRUGGLES / CONFLICTS
SIXES			
BALANCE / CHARITY / HAVING ENOUGH / GIVING/RECEIVING / LOOKED AFTER	SUCCESS / VICTORY / PRAISE / BALANCED EGO / TRIUMPH	NOSTALGIA / REUNIONS / MEMORIES / PAST EXPERIENCES / PLAYFULNESS	FINDING BALANCE / STAGNATION / MOVING FORWARD / DEPRESSION / LEARNING TO COPE
SEVENS			
ASSESSING / ACHIEVING GOALS / CHANGE DIRECTION / EVALUATION / CROSSROADS	COURAGE / DETERMINATION / SELF ASSERTION / DETERMINATION / STRENGTH	OPEN OPTIONS / UP IN THE AIR / LET GO / DECISIONS / PROCRASTINATING	BEING ALOOF / AVOIDANCE / EASY WAY OUT / STRATEGIES NEEDED / HIDING THE TRUTH
EIGHTS			
NEW SKILLS / RESULTS / DILIGENCE / METHODICAL / FINER DETAILS	TAKE ACTION / NECESSARY CHANGE / FAST ACTION / SPONTENEITY / SUDDEN CHANGE	LOSS OF INTEREST / CLOSURE REQUIRED / NEED TO WALK AWAY / MOVING ON / GIVING UP	FEELING TRAPPED / BOUND BY FEAR / POWERLESS / CONFUSION / OVERWHELMED
NINES			
INDEPENDENCE / SELF DISCIPLINE / COMFORT / SELF RELIANCE / SELF CONTROL	BEING DEFENSIVE / STRENGTH OF WILL / HEALING / PERSEVERENCE / PRECAUTIONS	ACHIEVEMENT / SELF SATISFACTION / AT PEACE / CONTENTMENT / SUCCESS	FEARS & WORRIES / FEELINGS OF GUILT / DEPRESSION / DISTRESS / ANXIETY
TENS			
SECURITY / SUCCESS / FAMILY / FONUDATIONS / ABUNDANCE	OVER BURDENED / UPHILL BATTLE / RESPONSABILITIES / PUSHING THROUGH / LEARNING TO SAY NO	LASTING HAPPINESS / BLESSINGS / HARMONY / FAMILY SUPPORT / FINDING PEACE	MISERY / ROCK BOTTOM / BEING THE VICTIM / SELF PITY / BEING WALKED OVER

RIDER-SMITH – COURT CARDS

PENTACLES	WANDS	CUPS	SWORDS
PAGES			
NEW IDEAS PRACTICALITY REALISM CREDIBILITY PROSPERITY	CHANGE DIRECTION DIFFERENT APPROACH WORTH THE RISK BE ASSERTIVE TACKLING CHALLENGES	TRUE FEELINGS RENEWAL TRUST INSTINCTS INNER GUIDANCE HANDLE WITH CARE	ANALYSE SPEAK DIRECTLY THINK FIRST RESEARCH BE PREPARED
KNIGHTS			
STEADY PROGRESS NEW CHALLENGES LOGIC REASONING EXAMINE ALL ANGLES	TRAVEL DARING PRESUMPTUOS TIME FOR CHANGE PROGRESS	OFFERS BEING MADE EMPHASISED FEELINGS TIME FOR TACT BE UNDERSTANDING INTROSPECTION	CHANGE OF EVENTS FULL KNOWLEDGE CLEAR REASONING BE ANALYTICAL PRIORITISE
QUEENS			
SENSIBLE ACHIEVEMENTS SELF CARING INDEPENDENCE ACCOMPLISHMENT	ACHIEVEMENT NOT HOLDING BACK SELF ASSURANCE HAVING FAITH DEDICATION	AVOID HARSHNESS TRUST INTUITION SHOW COMPASSION BE ACCEPTING SEEK THE SPIRITUAL	OPPORTUNITIES QUICK DECISION FACE THE TRUTH STICK TO THE RULES TIMES FOR HONESTY
KINGS			
CAUTION COMMITMENT STABILITY SECURITY MONEY SKILLS	INNOVATION TAKING THE LEAD MAKING A MOVE COURAGOUS NEW STRATEGIES	SEEK BETTER ADVICE FAIRNESS IS NEEDED BE OPEN MINDED PATIENCE IS NEEDED DIPLOMACY	CHANGE PROFESSION NEW PERSPECTIVE BE ANALYTICAL MAINTAIN MORALS HIGHER STANDARDS

THE FOOL	**THE MAGICIAN**	**HIGH PRIESTESS**	**THE EMPRESS**
SPONTANEITY NEW START LEAP OF FAITH FOOLISHNESS INNOCENCE	INDEPENDANCE INFINITE POWER HAVING PURPOSE MANIFESTING POTENTIAL	WISDOM BALANCE KNOWLEDGE INNER GUIDANCE INTUITION	FERTILITY NURTURING GROWTH MOTHER FIGURE VIBRANT HEALTH
THE EMPEROR	**THE HIEROPHANT**	**THE LOVERS**	**THE CHARIOT**
AUTHORITY ACCOMPLISHMENT FATHER FIGURE STRUCTURE CONFIDENCE	TRADITIONS DIVINE LAW CONFORMITY HERITAGE FAITH	SELF ESTABLISHMENT DECISIONS PERSONAL BELIEFS UNIONS RELATING TO OTHERS	CONFIDENCE TEST OF SKILLS SELF MASTERY DISCIPLINE AUTHORITY
STRENGTH	**THE HERMIT**	**WHEEL OF FORTUNE**	**JUSTICE**
INNER STRENGTH GENTLE APPROACH PERSEVERANCE ENDURANCE TRUIMPH	INNER KNOWLEDGE INTROSPECTION SPIRITUAL INSIGHT PERSONAL QUEST SPIRITUAL GUIDES	TURNING POINT DESTINY CHANGE ADVANCEMENT MIRACLES	JUSTICE FAIRNESS ETHICS RESPONSABILITY SEEING TRUTH
HANGED MAN	**DEATH**	**TEMPERENCE**	**THE DEVIL**
SELF AWARENESS SACRIFICES REFLECTION TURN AROUND GIVE UP CONTROL	NECESSARY CHANGE BIRTH/DEATH LETTING GO TRANSITIONING CYCLES	HARMONY BALANCE MODERATION COMPRIMISE RECOVERY	BOUND BY FEARS MATERIALISTIC ADDICTIONS SHADOW SELF DESPAIR
THE TOWER	**THE STAR**	**THE MOON**	**THE SUN**
NECESSARY CHAOS SUDDEN CHANGE DISRUPTED PLANS BEING HUMBLED TRANSFORMATION	OPTIMISM BLESSINGS FAITH SERENITY WISHES FULFILLED	PHOBIAS UNREALISTIC PIPE DREAMS FEELING LOST LACKING CONTROL	ENERGISED ENLIGHTENMENT VITALITY ENTHUSIASM FREEDOM
JUDGMENT	**THE WORLD**		
FRESH START REVELATION ABSOLUTION RENEWED HOPE RELEASING GUILT	 COMPLETION PERFECTION END RESULT CLOSURE PEACE OF MIND		

RIDER-SMITH – GREATER ARCANA

THE ART OF TAROT GUIDEBOOK

THOTH, CROWLEY – MINOR ARCANA

DISKS	WANDS	CUPS	SWORDS
ACES  MATERIAL GAIN / POWER / LABOUR / WEALTH / CONTENTMENT	ENERGY / STRENGTH / ROOT OF POWER / NATURAL FORCE / SEXUAL VIGOR	FERTILITY / PRODUCTIVITY / BEAUTY / PLEASURE / HAPPINESS	INVOKED FORCE / CONQUEST / ACTIVITY / JUST PUNISHMENT / TROUBLED
TWOS  CHANGE / HARMONY / LOSS & GAIN / WEAK & STRONG / INDUSTRIOUS	DOMINION / FORCE OF ENERGY / HARMONY IN POWER / BOLDNESS / FIERCENESS	HARMONY / RADIANT JOY / PLEASURE / WARM FRIENDSHIPS / CARELESSNESS	PEACE / DUAL NATURE / SACRIFICE / FINDING PLEASURE / INDECISION
THREES  WORK ENDEVOURS / BUSINESS / COMMERCIAL TRADE / START OF PROJECTS / SELFISH NATURE	VIRTUE / STRENGTH / ARROGANCE / REALIZATION OF HOPE / CONCEIT	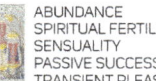 ABUNDANCE / SPIRITUAL FERTILITY / SENSUALITY / PASSIVE SUCCESS / TRANSIENT PLEASURE	SORROW / MELANCHOLY / UNHAPPINESS / DISRUPTION / ABSENCE
FOURS POWER / LAW & ORDER / GAIN OF MONEY / GAINING INFLUENCE / DOMINION / SUSPICION	COMPLETION / CONCLUSIONS / KNOWLEDGE / UNRELIABLE OUTCOME / OVERZEALOUSNESS	LUXURY / WEAKNESS / ABONDONMENT / ANXIETY IN PLEASURE / INJUSTICE	 TRUCE / REST FROM SORROW / RELIEF FOR ANXIETY / RECOVERY / CONVENTION
FIVES WORRY / INTENSE STRAIN / INACTIVITY / FINANCIAL LOSS / SETBACKS	STRIFE / QUARRELING / FIGHTING / COMPETITION / VIOLENCE	DISAPPOINTMENT / DISTURBANCE / MISFORTUNE / HEARTACHE / BETRAYAL	DEFEAT / LOSS / DISHONOUR / MALICE / WEAKNESS
SIXES SUCCESS / MATERIAL GAIN / INFLUENCE / POWER / INSOLENCE	 VICTORY / BALANCE ENERGY / GAIN / SUCCESS / INSOLENCE	PLEASURE / WELL-BEING / EFFORTLESS HARMONY / SATISFACTION / HAPPINESS	SCIENCE / DIRECT INTELLIGENCE / LABOUR / WATER JOURNEY / CONCEITED
SEVENS FAILURE / UNFINISHED WORK / UNMET GOALS / DELAYED GROWTH / DECEIT	 HONOUR / STRUGGLES / SMALL VICTORIES / COURAGE / QUARRELING	DELUSION / ILLUSION OF SUCCESS / ADDICTIONS / INTOXICATION / UNFULFILLED PROMISES	 FUTILITY / UNSTABLE EFFORT / STRIVING IN VAIN / INCOMPLETION / EXHAUSTION
EIGHTS PRUDENCE / MATERIAL SMARTS / BUILDING / CUNNING / AVARICE	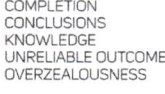 SWIFTNESS / LIGHT / HIGH ENERGY / APROACHING GOALS / FREEDOM	INDOLENCE / ABANDONED SUCCESS / DECLINING INTEREST / INSTABILITY / TEMPORARY SUCCESS	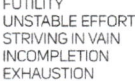 INTERFERENCE / MIDIRECTED ENERGY / NEGLECT / BAD LUCK / UNSEEN EVENTS
NINES GOOD FORTUNE / INHERITANCE / IMPROVED WEALTH / ENVY / LOSS	STRENGTH / POWER / RECOVERY / STABILITY / HEALTH	 HAPPINESS / COMPLETE SUCCESS / PLEASURE / PHYSICAL WELL-BEING / VANITY	CRUELTY / MENTAL ANGUISH / DESPAIR / SUFFERING / ILLNESS
TENS WEALTH / PROSPERITY / CREATIVITY / LAZINESS / DULLNESS	 OPPRESSION / DETACH FROM SPIRIT / DESTRUCTIVE ENERGY / SLANDER / SELFISHNESS	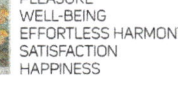 CONTENTMENT / PURSUIT OF PLEASURE / DESIRED OUTCOMES / PEACEMAKING / DISSIPATION	 RUIN / FAULTY REASONING / FAILURE / DISRUPTION / DEATH

THOTH, CROWLEY – COURT CARDS

DISKS	WANDS	CUPS	SWORDS
PRINCESSES			
STRONG, GENEROUS, DILIGENT, WASTEFUL, BENEVOLENT	ENERGETIC, INDIVUALISTIC, DARING, EXPRESSIVE, SUPERFICIAL	GRACIOUS, SWEET, GENTLE, INDOLENT, SELFISH	STERN, REVENGEFUL, DESTRUCTIVE LOGIC, AGGRESSIVE, MANIPULATIVE
PRINCES			
ENERGETIC, STEADFAST, COMPETENT, DULL, SKEPTICAL OF SPIRIT	SWIFT / STRONG, IMPULSIVE, GENEROUS, VIOLENT, NOBLE/JUST	SECRET VIOLENCE, INTENSE PASSION, ARTISTIC, AMBITIOUS, RUTHLESS	INTELLECTUAL, FULL OF IDEAS, DOMINEERING, INTENSELY CLEVER, MALICIOUS
QUEENS			
AMBITOUS, AFFECTIONATE, CHARMING, TIMID, FOOLISH	ADAPTABLE, PERSISTENT ENERGY, CALM AUTHORITY, POWER OF ATTRACTION, INTOLERANT	OBERSEVER, DREAMY, TRANQUIL, IMAGINATIVE, PASSIVE	GRACEFUL, PERCEPTIVE, KEEN OBSERVER, CONFIDENT, CRUEL
KNIGHTS			
PATIENT, LABOUROUS, MATERIAL FOCUS, PETTY, JEALOUS	ACTIVE, GENEROUS, SWIFTNESS, PROUD, CRUELTY	COMMITMENT ISSUES, AMIABLE BUT PASSIVE, UNSUSTAINABLE, SHALLOW, UNTRUTHFUL	SKILLFUL, CLEVER, FIERCE, COURAGOUS, DECEITFUL

THE FOOL FRESH IDEAS, TRANCENDENTAL, ECCENTRICITY, IMPULSIVENESS, FOLLY	**THE MAGUS** SKILLS, WISDOM, CUNNING, DECEIT, ESOTERIC POWER	**THE PRIESTESS** ALTERATION, BALANCE, PURE INFLUENCE, LIFES EBB/FLOW, CHANGE	**THE EMPRESS** BEAUTY, HAPPINESS, PLEASURE, GOOD FORTUNE, GENTLENESS
THE EMPEROR CONQUEST, STRIFE, STABILITY, AMBITION, GOVERNMENTS	**THE HIEROPHANT** DIVINE WISDOM, STUBBORN STRENGTH, ENDURANCE, TEACHING, ORGANIZATIONS	**THE LOVERS** INSPIRATION, INTUITION, INTELLIGENCE, ATTRACTION, LOVE	**THE CHARIOT** TRIUMPH, VICTORY, OBEDIENCE, FAITHFULNESS, SUCCESS
ADJUSTMENT JUSTICE, BALANCE, SUSPENDING ACTION, LAWSUITS, CONTRACTS	**THE HERMIT** INWARD ILLUMINATION, DIVINE INSPIRATION, WISDOM, CONTEMPLATIOM, RETIREMENT	**FORTUNE** CHANGE IN FORTUNE, DESTINY, GOOD LUCK	**LUST** COURAGE, STRENGTH, MAGIC POWER, LIFE FORCE, CONTROL
THE HANGED MAN REDEMPTION, SACRIFICE, NEW PERSPECTIVE, PUNISHMENT, SUFFERING	**DEATH** TRANSFORMATION, CHANGE, SUDDEN CHANGES, ILLUSORY DEATH, DESTRUCTIVE RELEASE	**ART** COMBINING FORCES, REALIZATIONS, ECONOMY, MANAGMENT, ESCAPE	**THE DEVIL** BLIND IMPULSE, UNSCRUPULOUS, TEMPTATION, OBSESSIONS, DISCONTENTMENT
THE TOWER QUARREL, COMBAT, DESTRUCTION, SUDDEN DEATH, AMBITION	**THE STAR** UNEXPECTED HELP, HOPE, CLEAR VISION, SPIRITUAL INSIGHTS, DREAMINESS	**THE MOON** ILLUSION, DECEPTION, FALSEHOOD, VOLUNTARY CHANGE, HYSTERIA	**THE SUN** GLORY, RICHES, PLEASURE, ARROGANCE, MANIFESTATION
THE AEON CLOSURE, RESOLUTION, DEFINITIVE ACTION, END OF AN AGE, START OF AN ERA	**THE UNIVERSE** SYNTHESIS, DELAYS, COMPLETION, PERSEVERANCE, CLEAR THINKING		

THOTH, CROWLEY – MAJOR ARCANA

Chapter 8

Tarot Through the Sephirotic Tree

Note on Systems and Alignment

The Tree of Life, or Sephirotic Tree, is a structure found in the Kabbalistic tradition. It's been carried into Western esoteric practice, including Tarot, and is often used as a framework to understand the flow of energy from spiritual to physical. Over time, it's been mapped onto the Tarot system in various ways. In the Golden Dawn tradition, which played a significant role in shaping modern Tarot, the Court Cards were associated with specific elements in a particular order: Kings were Fire, Queens were Water, Knights were Air and Pages were Earth. In the RWS tradition, however, the elemental structure is slightly different. The Knights are Fire and the Kings are Air, while the Queens and Pages remain as Water and Earth, respectively.

Since this guidebook follows the RWS system, that structure is the one used throughout this chapter. Where relevant, older associations are acknowledged so that you can understand the wider context, but the teachings here are written to support the elemental and symbolic structure of the RWS tradition.

Understanding the Tree of Life

The Tree of Life is made up of ten spheres, called Sephirot, and twenty-two connecting paths. These spheres represent stages or aspects of consciousness, divine expression or states of being. The paths between them show how these aspects relate to one another. The Tree is usually shown with three vertical columns and four horizontal levels. It can be helpful to view it as a descending process - a movement from source or divine spark into embodied life - but it's not a fixed or linear ladder. The structure is symbolic. It's a pattern we move within, not something we climb once and never return to. You may revisit different stages of growth, circle back to earlier insights or find yourself integrating something from the center before addressing what's below.

There's an important symbiotic relationship between all parts of the Tree, just like there is between all parts of the Tarot. Even though the Major Arcana can be seen as a journey from The Fool to The World, it isn't a one-directional path. Tarot asks you to meet yourself where you are - not just at one fixed point, but across many layers. The Tree of Life does the same.

The Three Pillars

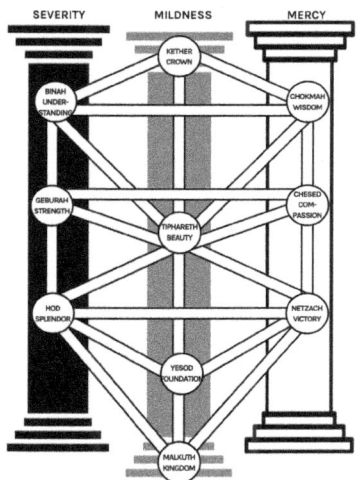

The Sephirotic Tree with Pillars

The Tree is structured into three vertical columns or energetic streams called pillars. Each pillar reflects a distinct current of energy, and although they appear as separate paths, they are always in relationship. You're not meant to walk just one - they move through you, and your work is often to notice which is speaking louder at a given time and how that affects your choices, thoughts and internal responses.

The Pillar of Severity is on the left. It represents structure, discipline, discernment and restraint. It includes the spheres of Binah, Geburah and Hod - qualities that help define, contain and challenge us. In Tarot, this stream of energy is reflected in moments that require boundaries, clarity or refinement. It often appears when something is being narrowed, shaped or tested and asks for precision, responsibility or the courage to say no.

The Pillar of Mercy is on the right. It holds qualities of expansion, compassion, creativity and flow. It includes Chokmah, Chesed and Netzach - expressions of intuitive growth, generosity and emotional openness. When this stream is reflected in Tarot, it often brings energy that supports trust, movement and wholehearted expression. It reminds you where things want to open and where softness or courage can create meaningful change.

The Pillar of Balance is in the centre. It is the path of integration and spiritual alignment, including Keter, Tiphereth, Yesod and Malkuth - a vertical line that carries energy from potential into presence. This pillar helps you connect extremes, hold multiple truths at once and remain grounded while moving through inner change. In Tarot, this often shows up as the quiet center - the space where your insight deepens, where you pause and realign or where something falls into place after a period of dissonance.

All three pillars are always at work. Like the interplay of suits or the way positions in a spread relate to one another, the pillars are best understood in conversation, not in isolation. The task is not to favor one or reject another, but to observe their interaction and notice where something is overactive, underdeveloped or ready to be brought into greater balance.

The Ten Sephirot

Each of the ten Sephirot represents a distinct quality or state of energy. These are not steps in a fixed sequence, but active principles that shape how we experience the world - spiritually, emotionally, mentally and physically. When working with Tarot, the Sephirot can help you understand the core energy behind each number in the Minor Arcana, giving you a way to read not just what a card says, but how it functions within a wider process of growth or contraction.

1. **Keter - Crown**
   Keter is pure being - the origin point, the divine spark before form. In the Minor Arcana, this echoes in the Aces. Each Ace carries the full, undivided essence of its suit - the potential for fire, water, air or earth, before that energy is shaped by experience. Aces are not outcomes - they are openings, the first breath of what may come.
2. **Chokmah - Wisdom**
   Chokmah is dynamic force, creative impulse and the instinct to act before thinking. It reflects raw movement, often without form or definition. The twos in Tarot begin to show this current - the split from oneness into duality, tension, polarity or connection. It is the moment where energy starts to move into relationship.
3. **Binah - Understanding**
   Binah contains what Chokmah releases. It is structure, boundary and the beginning of form. The threes often reflect synthesis - not just two parts held in contrast,

but a third perspective, resolution or direction. There is pattern here, and the capacity to define and hold something in place.

4. **Chesed - Compassion**

   Chesed is abundance, expansion and generosity. It moves outward and supports growth. The fours in Tarot often carry this energy through stability, order or a sense of anchoring. Here we find a resting point - the structure is set and things can begin to root or grow into something deeper.

5. **Geburah - Strength**

   Geburah is the counterforce to Chesed. It's the necessary restriction, the limit, the edge that calls for honesty. The fives in Tarot often speak to challenge, confrontation or loss - not to harm, but to show where something is being tested. This is where the structure gets questioned. Growth requires pressure.

6. **Tiphereth - Beauty**

   Tiphereth is the heart of the Tree. It holds integration, truth and alignment with what is real. The sixes often reflect a return to balance, a sense of harmony or meaningful exchange. This is where a deeper order re-emerges after disruption - the point of reconnection, where insight meets clarity.

7. **Netzach - Victory**

   Netzach is emotional movement, desire, persistence and the pull of the heart. The sevens in Tarot often show struggle, pressure or the need to hold your ground. There's energy here, but also uncertainty - a test of will or inner clarity. It's where you ask, "Do I continue? Is this worth it?" and choose to move forward or redirect.

8. **Hod – Splendor**
   Hod holds the structure of thought - intellect, logic, communication. It follows Netzach and asks, "What do I know? What makes sense?" The eights reflect clarity, momentum, and movement - sometimes mental, sometimes practical. Hod refines the emotional fire of Netzach into something that can be communicated or applied.

9. **Yesod – Foundation**
   Yesod is the energetic blueprint. It holds memory, patterns, dreams and the filter through which higher energies pass into form. The nines in Tarot reflect culmination - not completion, but the full weight of what has been built. This is where integration happens. You feel the stretch before something is made real.

10. **Malkuth – Kingdom**
    Malkuth is the world made manifest - the body, the present moment, the lived experience. The tens in Tarot are the result: what becomes of the idea, the desire, the thought, the feeling, when it has fully landed? Sometimes it's fulfilment. Sometimes it's heaviness. But always, it is real - grounded, final and ready to return to the beginning.

Each number in the Minor Arcana can be read through this lens, not as fixed definitions, but as energetic qualities. The suit provides the context - fire, water, air or earth - and the number shows what stage of movement or expression is being revealed. Together, they reflect not just what is happening, but what kind of energy is present, where it's heading and what it's asking of you.

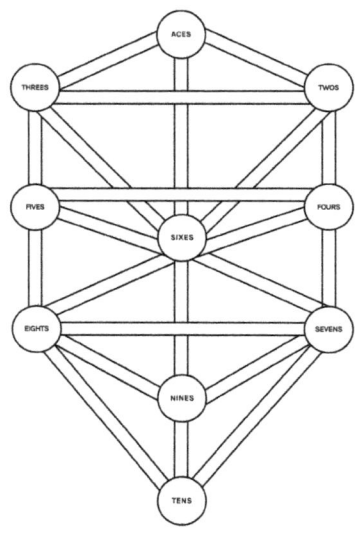

The Ten Sephirot

The Four Worlds

In Kabbalistic teaching, all manifestation takes place through Four Worlds which are considered the stages of descent from spirit into form. These worlds also correspond with the Suits in Tarot.

- Atziluth is the World of Emanation. It is aligned with fire and represents divine will, spiritual essence and the first spark before form. It corresponds with the Suit of Wands.
- Briah is the World of Creation. It is associated with water, emotion and the realm of intuition and archetype. It relates to the Suit of Cups.
- Yetzirah is the World of Formation. This is the domain of thought, communication and structure - the formation of ideas. It is connected to air and the Suit of Swords.
- Assiah is the World of Action. This is the physical world, where ideas and energy become tangible. It corresponds with earth and the Suit of Pentacles.

These worlds are sometimes shown as layers placed over the Tree of Life, with Atziluth at the top and Assiah at the bottom. While this image can be helpful, it's important not to take it too literally. The Four Worlds are not strict zones or stages, they are interwoven aspects of the process of becoming. They give us insight into which layer of reality we're working with, whether inspiration, feeling, thought or action.

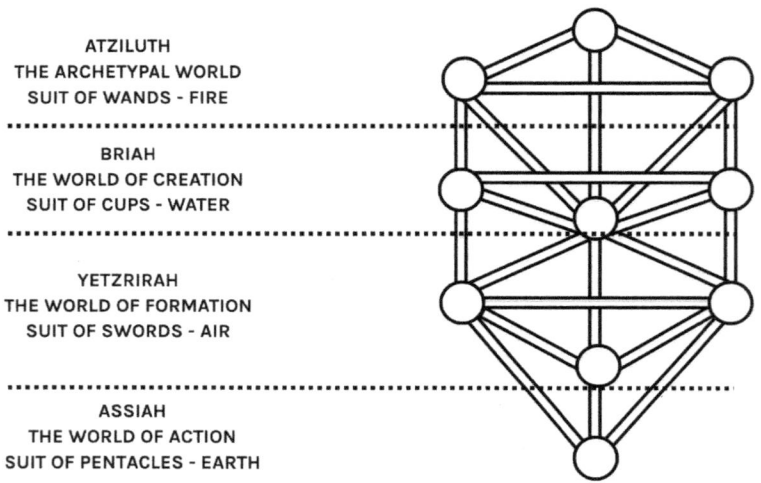

The Four Worlds

The Court Cards and Four Worlds

There are different ways that people have linked the Court Cards to the Four Worlds. In older traditions, the four ranks - King, Queen, Knight and Page, were mapped directly onto the Four Worlds in a fixed hierarchy. But that structure doesn't match the RWS system, especially when you consider the RWS elemental associations. Rather than trying to fit each Court rank into a specific world, it's more useful to look at the Suits and their elements as the guiding principle. The Suits themselves correspond to the Four Worlds, and the Court Cards within those suits represent different expressions of that energy.

- The suit of Wands is aligned with fire and with Atziluth. The Knight of Wands shows fire in motion - drive, action and bold energy. The Queen of Wands holds the intuitive, magnetic power of fire. The King of Wands expresses leadership, vision and the ability to inspire. The Page of Wands brings enthusiasm, curiosity and the first spark of movement or creative impulse.
- The suit of Cups relates to water and Briah. The Knight of Cups is emotional energy seeking expression - romantic, idealistic and sometimes impulsive. The Queen of Cups reflects emotional depth, sensitivity and spiritual receptivity. The King of Cups holds emotional maturity and the ability to remain steady in deep feeling. The Page of Cups represents the beginning of emotional awareness - wonder, intuition and imaginative insight.
- The suit of Swords corresponds to air and Yetzirah. The Knight of Swords is swift, direct and mentally focused - often rushing in with a sharp idea or pointed intention. The Queen of Swords uses clarity and discernment to set boundaries and cut through confusion. The King of Swords holds the mental command of air - logical, reasoned, strategic. The Page of Swords is the curious, watchful learner - gathering knowledge and testing understanding.
- The suit of Pentacles is aligned with earth and Assiah. The Knight of Pentacles is methodical, consistent and devoted to the task at hand. The Queen of Pentacles offers care, stability and a strong relationship to the physical world. The King of Pentacles shows grounded

authority, leadership in the material realm and long-term vision. The Page of Pentacles begins the journey of learning how to turn knowledge into something real - planting seeds, committing to growth and paying attention to what matters.

Each of the Court Cards expresses its element in a slightly different way. When you see them in a reading, think about how the suit's energy is showing up: is it moving fast, held with inner strength, being expressed outwardly or just beginning to stir? The Four Worlds can help you sense which layer that energy is working through - whether it's still in thought, already in motion or coming into the physical.

The Twenty-Two Paths

Between the ten Sephirot on the Tree of Life are twenty-two connecting lines. These are known as the paths, and each one represents a movement - a process of development, refinement or transformation between two states of consciousness. While the Sephirot reflect core energies or qualities, the paths reflect how those energies interact and what happens in between.

Each of the twenty-two paths corresponds with a letter of the Hebrew alphabet and has been traditionally matched with one of the Major Arcana cards. These cards reflect key archetypes and lessons - not just stages of life, but states of mind, turning points and deeper internal shifts. When placed on the Tree, they can help illuminate the type of work being done between two spheres. The path of The Hermit, for example, shows the process of moving from reflection into illumination. The path of The Lovers can reflect the integration of choice, connection or internal harmony. Each path is its own teaching.

There are different versions of which card belongs to which path - most commonly based on Golden Dawn attributions - but the aim here is not to memorize a fixed map. Rather, it's to understand that each Major Arcana card represents a kind of bridging process. The paths are not steps in a strict order. They can be walked in many different ways. They may appear one at a time or several at once. Some may repeat, others may feel unfamiliar.

Working with the Major Arcana on the Tree is not about trying to place yourself in one spot and stay there. It's about seeing which energies are in dialogue in your life and which internal movements are taking place. If you find yourself drawing several Majors in a reading, you might consider how they connect as paths - what inner work might be unfolding between seemingly opposite or complementary forces. What are you being asked to navigate? What is being reconciled? What insight is trying to emerge through this specific path?

The Tree gives shape to the internal terrain. The Major Arcana gives you language and symbols to work with it. Used together, they offer a way to trace not just where you are, but how you're changing - and what deeper story is being told through your experiences.

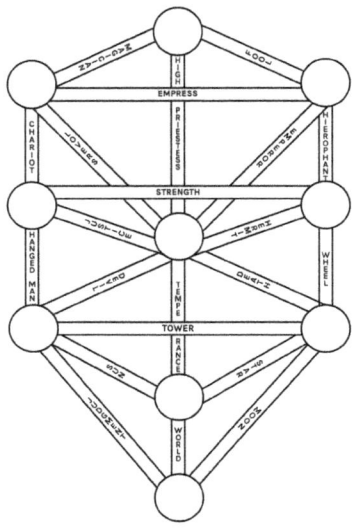

The 22 Paths

Using The Tree for Self Development

The Sephirotic Tree becomes truly valuable when it's applied with intention. It's not just a map of divine emanations or mystical concepts - it's a tool for reflecting on your own inner world. It can help you identify where you are, what may be calling for attention and which qualities are asking to be strengthened, softened or integrated.

You might find yourself caught in thought (Hod), circling the same mental patterns, while neglecting action or emotional movement (Netzach). You might be overextending in generosity (Chesed), forgetting to honor boundaries and discernment (Geburah). Or perhaps you're deep in subconscious cycles (Yesod), unsure how to anchor them into real, grounded change (Malkuth).

The Tree allows you to locate yourself in a way that isn't static or prescriptive. It doesn't label you - it reflects you. It invites you to hold the complexity of your experience, to see not just the symptom but the energetic pattern beneath it. Every sphere on the Tree offers a lens, and every path between them offers an insight into how movement happens - sometimes with ease, sometimes through pressure, sometimes through stillness.

The Tarot works in much the same way. It meets you in your moment and shows you something about your state of being, your internal dynamics or your larger arc of growth. When used alongside the Tree, the cards give voice to the energies within the structure. A numbered card might reflect the quality of a specific Sephirah within a suit's domain. A Court Card might show you how that energy is being expressed. A Major Arcana card might mirror a deeper process between two aspects of the self - a path you're walking internally, consciously or not.

Both systems are often mistaken as linear frameworks - a spiritual ladder or a hero's journey from beginning to end. But the truth is, they are cyclical, layered and often deeply personal. The Major Arcana has a sequence, yes, but no card exists in isolation, and the journey through them rarely happens in a straight line. Likewise, the Tree has an order, but it's not a strict ascent or descent. It is a living map. You may find yourself looping back through familiar places with new awareness. You may feel pulled in multiple directions at once. You may move horizontally instead of upward - not because you're lost, but because something vital is unfolding across dimensions that you can't fully see yet.

The Tree and the Tarot are not systems to master. They are companions to walk with. They offer structure, but not confinement. They offer insight, not instruction. And when used together, they create a layered language of transformation - one that doesn't force a conclusion, but helps you become more present, more honest and more awake to what's really happening.

These tools don't give you the answers. They help you ask better questions. And in the space that opens between question and insight, something powerful begins to shift.

Chapter 9

The Major Arcana

The Major Arcana consists of twenty-two cards and is considered the heart and soul of the Tarot. In most decks, it begins with the Fool at zero and ends with the World at twenty-one. These cards depict universal aspects of human nature and fundamental life experiences. Each card carries a name and a numeral, with some directly representing concepts such as Justice or Judgment, others embodying personality archetypes like The High Priestess or the Emperor and some reflecting approaches to life, such as the Hierophant or the Magician. The remainder symbolize celestial bodies, including the Sun, the Moon and the Star - representing cosmic forces; while others portray transformational experiences, such as Death and the Chariot.

When Major Arcana cards appear in a reading, they highlight pivotal moments and deeper life themes, acting as signposts along one's path. Their presence often signifies significant lessons, crossroads or personal transformations. The Major Arcana is frequently referred to as the Fool's Journey - a symbolic representation of the soul's evolution through life's trials, wisdom gained and eventual mastery. Though the imagery and names may vary between different Tarot traditions, the underlying journey remains universal.

Unlike the Minor Arcana, which deals with everyday experiences and external circumstances, the Major Arcana reveals the deeper patterns of self-discovery, personal growth and spiritual development. These cards represent the profound shifts that shape one's existence. Some of these transformations may be subtle, while others can be life-altering. When working with the Tarot, particularly with the Major Arcana, one engages with a powerful system of archetypal wisdom that can serve as both a mirror and a guide.

A Journey through the Majors

The journey through the Major Arcana presented in this section is my own take on the soul's journey. It is based on my work with psychology, human nature, esoteric teachings and the commonalities between them. This perspective integrates these different influences to provide a structured yet fluid framework for working with the cards as a tool for self-understanding and transformation.

This journey can be viewed in seven key stages, each representing a phase of personal growth and evolution:

1. The Self – Understanding the foundation of identity and personal potential.
2. Preconditioning – Examining societal and familial influences that shape beliefs and behaviors.

3. Knowledge of Self – Establishing personal values, ethics and self-awareness.
4. Lessons – Facing inner and outer challenges that test one's character and resilience.
5. Attainments – Achieving inner peace, wisdom and enlightenment through lived experience.
6. Revelation – Recognizing profound truths that reshape perception and understanding.
7. Mastery – Embracing completion while recognizing that the journey is cyclical and ever-unfolding.

Each card within these sections represents a unique experience, lesson or area for growth. Understanding where each card falls within this framework allows for a more holistic approach to Tarot study and self-exploration. The journey through the Major Arcana is more cyclical than linear, and one may revisit different stages at various points in life, learning deeper lessons each time.

The Major Arcana is not just a structured narrative; it is a deeply personal journey that reflects individual experiences, challenges and transformations. This is the approach I use in tarot therapy, personal readings and my teaching sessions - working with these cards as a method of self-development rather than just as divinatory tools. Each of us moves through these stages at our own pace, sometimes revisiting earlier lessons before moving forward. The cards do not dictate a strict path; rather, they illuminate the lessons we are currently encountering and provide insight into the energies shaping our reality.

Tarot is an experiential tool, and the Major Arcana is particularly profound when applied to personal exploration. The key is to work with the cards in a way that resonates with your own journey - identifying how they align with personal experiences, emotional shifts and periods of transformation. By viewing them through this lens, Tarot becomes not just a symbolic language but a practical framework for understanding the self, processing life's challenges and experiences and embracing personal evolution.

From here, the journey begins with the self, the foundation upon which all other growth is built. This section covers the Fool, the Magician, and the High Priestess - each representing different aspects of authenticity, personal power and inner wisdom. Before one can navigate the external world, it is crucial to explore the internal one, reconnecting with the essence of who they truly are.

JOURNEY THROUGH THE MAJOR ARCANA

THE SELF
THE SOUL | KNOWLEDGE | WISDOM

PRE-CONDITIONING
COMPASSION | DISCPLINE | HERITAGE

KNOWLEDGE OF SELF
ESTABLISHING SELF | SELF MASTERY | FORTITUDE

LESSONS
SPIRITUALITY | CHANGE | MORALITY | PRUDENCE | LETTING GO
SHADOW SELF | BALANCE | TRANSFORMATION

ACHIEVEMENTS
PEACE | INTUITION | ENLIGHTENMENT

REVELATION
ATONEMENT

MASTERY
COMPLETION

THE SOUL	BEGINNING | FREE SPIRIT | LEAP OF FAITH
KNOWLEDGE	POWER | PURPOSE | CREATION
WISDOM	KNOWLEDGE | INTUITION | GUIDANCE
COMPASSION	FERTILITY | NURTURING | ABUNDANCE
DISCPLINE	AUTHORITY | STRUCTURE | ORDER
HERITAGE	TRADITIONS | ANCESTRY | CULTURE
ESTABLISHING SELF	CORE MORALS | BELIEFS | INTIMACY
SELF MASTERY	COMMITMENT | DETERMINATION | TENACITY
FORTITUDE	PERSEVERANCE | ENDURANCE | ASSERTIVENES
SPIRITUALITY	INSIGHT | SPIRIT GUIDE | SPIRIT QUEST
CHANGE	FATE | DESTINY | ADVANCEMENT
MORALITY	TRUTH | ETHICS | RESPONSABILITY
PRUDENCE	INSIGHT | REFLECTING | SACRIFICE
LETTING GO	ENDINGS | TRANSITIONING | RENEWAL
BALANCE	HARMONY | MODERATION | RECOVERY
SHADOW SELF	DESPAIR | ADDICTIONS | FEAR
TRANSFORMATION	CHAOS | UPHEAVAL | AWAKENING
PEACE	RENEWAL | SERENITY | MINDFULNESS
INTUITION	DREAMTIME | SECRETS | SUBCONSCIOUS
ENLIGHTENMENT	ENERGY | VITALITY | AWARENESS
ATONEMENT	REBIRTH | ABSOLUTION | RELEASING GUILT
COMPLETION	END RESULT | SATISFACTION | ATTAINMENT

The Self

This section explores the three cards that represent the self: the Fool, the Magician and the High Priestess. Together, they form the foundation of identity and self-awareness within the journey of the Major Arcana.

The Fool embodies the unconditioned self - free, authentic and untouched by external expectations. He moves through life with trust, unburdened by stress or limitation, guided by an innate understanding that the only true necessities are food, water and shelter. Everything beyond that is an added layer, often complicating what is otherwise simple. The Fool is not reckless but open, embracing the unknown with the wisdom that experience itself is the path.

The Magician and the High Priestess represent two essential aspects of the self - knowledge and wisdom. The Magician is the active force, the power to create, manifest and shape reality through skill and awareness. He represents external mastery - the ability to harness mind, body, emotions and energy with intent. The High Priestess, in contrast, is the passive force, the deep well of inner knowing, intuition and connection to the unseen. She embodies internal mastery - the ability to navigate stillness, listen to what lies beyond perception and trust in higher awareness. The Magician is yang, the High Priestess is yin. Together, they balance the dynamic and receptive aspects of personal power.

Self-awareness is the foundation of any spiritual journey. It is the ability to witness yourself without judgment, to see beyond thoughts, emotions and conditioning. Nothing is missing -

you are already whole. Yet, through life's experiences and external influences, layers of preconditioning can obscure the truth of who you are. The path is not about acquiring something new but about remembering, about peeling back these layers to reveal the wisdom, power and authenticity that have always been present. The Fool, the Magician and the High Priestess serve as guides in this process, reminding you of the self that exists beneath the noise - the self that has always been.

The Fool – A Foolish Journey

Imagine a newborn - pure, untouched by expectation, free from external influence. This is the Fool, the embodiment of raw authenticity. At birth, there are no conditioned beliefs, no imposed limitations - just an open, unfiltered experience of existence. The Fool represents the beginning of the journey, stepping off the proverbial cliff into life's unfolding experiences with trust and curiosity.

Throughout life, we encounter cycles of change and renewal - moments that call for us to embrace the unknown, start fresh and surrender to what lies ahead. The Fool reminds us that clarity and transformation often require a leap of faith, a willingness to move forward even when the path is unclear.

At its core, the Fool is about living in alignment with oneself, unbound by expectation or conformity. Society encourages adherence to predefined roles, but the true spiritual journey is about reclaiming authenticity. The Fool calls for a return to that raw, unfiltered state - to meet life with courage, curiosity and an open heart.

The Fool does not seek titles, achievements or external validation. His wisdom is in simply being - living rather than controlling, experiencing rather than resisting. To truly understand enlightenment, one must embrace the Fool's way of being - learning, growing and surrendering to the unpredictable flow of existence.

UNLIMITED POSSIBILITIES
SPONTANEITY
DOING THE UNEXPECTED
NEW BEGINNINGS, PHASE, PATH
LIVING IN THE MOMENT
HAVING FAITH
TRUSTING LIFE'S PROCESSES
BEING OPEN & RECEPTIVE
INNOCENCE & PURITY

HEADING INTO THE UNKNOWN
LEAP OF FAITH
FREEDOM TO DO OR BE ANYTHING

ADDITIONAL ASSOCIATIONS
CRYSTAL — GREEN TOURMALINE
ASTROLOGY — URANUS
ELEMENT — AIR
NUMEROLOGY — ZERO

The Fool meaning & associations

The Magician – The Magic Within

The Magician represents personal power - the ability to shape reality through intention, focus and mastery of one's tools. He is a reminder that you are a creator, fully capable of directing your energy to manifest what you need and desire. Holding the four elements - Pentacle (earth, material stability), Wand (fire, creative power), Cup (water, emotions and intuition) and Sword (air, intellect and clarity) - he embodies the fundamental forces of self-mastery.

Mastery begins with awareness. The Magician asks, "Are you consciously creating your life, or are you allowing others to shape it for you? Are you using your abilities wisely, or are they being misdirected?" Understanding and wielding these tools effectively is an essential part of the journey.

The Magician is action - the conscious application of knowledge to achieve transformation. He acknowledges that infinite potential lies within, but it is up to the individual to harness it. His lesson is one of empowerment - recognizing that you already possess everything needed to navigate life's challenges and carve your own path.

While the Fool is pure potential, the Magician is directed energy. He teaches that thought and action must align for true manifestation. Yet power without wisdom can lead to imbalance, and this is where the High Priestess enters the equation.

MASTERY OF SKILLS
UTILISING YOUR TALENTS
INDEPENDENCE
INFINITE POWER
HAVING PURPOSE
BEING COMMITTED
MAKING AN IMPACT
REALISING YOUR POTENTIAL
BEING CLEAR ABOUT YOUR INTENTIONS

ENTREPRENEURSHIP
CONSCIOUS AWARENESS

ADDITIONAL ASSOCIATIONS
CRYSTAL   - QUARTZ
ASTROLOGY   - MERCURY
ELEMENT   - AIR
NUMEROLOGY   - ONE

The Magician - meaning & associations

The High Priestess — A Higher Power

The High Priestess is the seat of inner wisdom, intuition and the subconscious mind. She is the part of the self that does not act impulsively but observes, understands and integrates. She represents the unseen - the mysteries beneath the surface - and the ability to trust in deeper knowledge.

Where the Magician commands external mastery, the High Priestess embodies internal mastery. She does not seek control over the world but moves in harmony with its natural flow. Her lessons are of patience, introspection and trust in the quiet voice within. She reminds you that there is more to existence than what is seen or logically understood. Holding the wisdom of past lessons and the power of intuition, she grants access to knowledge beyond reason.

She asks, "Are you listening to your inner guidance, or are you ignoring it? Are you trusting your deeper knowing, or are you searching for answers outside yourself?"

The balance between the Magician and the High Priestess creates a fully realized self. One without the other leads to imbalance - knowledge without wisdom is reckless, and intuition without action is stagnant. Together, they form the dual aspects of personal mastery.

Understanding these three archetypes - the Fool, the Magician and the High Priestess - lays the foundation for the journey ahead. They reveal that self-awareness, conscious action and deep intuition must work together to navigate the path authentically. The journey of self-discovery begins here, with the recognition that you already hold everything needed to walk your path with clarity and purpose.

WISDOM & INTUITION	ALLOWING THINGS TO BLOOM
ACHIEVING BALANCE	ACKNOWLEDGING SHADOWS
KNOWLEDGE OF THE UNKNOWN	KNOWN MYSTERIES
SUBCONSCIOUS AWARENESS	
BEING OPEN & RECEPTIVE	**ADDITIONAL ASSOCIATIONS**
TRUSTING YOUR INNER VOICE	CRYSTAL - AGATE GEODE
SEEKING INNER GUIDANCE	ASTROLOGY - MOON
SEEING BEYOND THE OBVIOUS	ELEMENT - WATER
UNDERSTANDING POSSIBILITIES	NUMEROLOGY - TWO

The High Priestess - meaning & associations

Pre-Conditioning

Pre-conditioning is where the real work begins. It is not a stage that is completed once and left behind but one that will be revisited throughout the journey. These pre-conditions are the external influences that have shaped who you believe yourself to be - your personality, behaviors, addictions, anxieties, beliefs and patterns. Yet these layers are not the core of who you truly are.

Pre-conditioning comes from upbringing, culture, society, education, traditions and personal experiences. These influences shape thoughts and behaviors, often without conscious awareness. The spiritual journey requires peeling back these layers, questioning what has been imposed and distinguishing between what is truly yours and what has simply been inherited.

This conditioning runs deep, influencing how you see yourself, how you react to the world and the choices you make. The three primary sources of conditioning are parental influence - maternal and paternal - and society, represented in the Tarot by the Empress, the Emperor and the Hierophant.

The Empress represents compassion and nurturing. This conditioning shapes how love is received and expressed, whether through warmth and care, or through a lack of it. Reflecting on experiences of compassion - both given and withheld - reveals patterns in how you relate to yourself and others. The Empress teaches the importance of cultivating a balanced and unconditional form of self-love, one not dependent on past validation or neglect.

The Emperor represents discipline and structure. While the form of discipline has evolved throughout history, its purpose remains the same - to guide, shape and instill order. Understanding how discipline was modeled is essential in developing a healthy relationship with self-motivation, decision-making and responsibility. A well-balanced sense of discipline brings focus and clarity, while imbalance can lead to either rigid control or complete lack of direction.

The Hierophant represents inherited beliefs, traditions and societal expectations. This conditioning is passed down through culture, religion and community. Many accept these influences without question, shaping their worldview according to what they have been taught. Examining these beliefs without attachment or judgment allows for clarity. Some aspects may align with the authentic self, while others may no longer serve a purpose.

Working through pre-conditioning brings a deeper understanding of the self. It reveals how external influences shape perception and behavior. This process is not about rejecting everything learned but about consciously choosing what aligns. The goal is to uncover the authentic self that has always been present beneath the layers of conditioning.

The Empress — The Gift of Compassion

The Empress embodies nurturing, unconditional love and the deep connection to life itself. She represents the first bond formed - the relationship with a mother or primary caregiver. This connection lays the foundation for how love, safety and emotional nourishment are experienced.

The Empress is not only an external influence but also an internal force - the ability to nurture and care for oneself. She is the aspect of self-compassion, self-care and personal growth. When balanced, she fosters healthy emotional connections and an openness to life's pleasures. However, when distorted by conditioning, this energy can manifest as difficulty receiving love, self-sacrifice to the point of depletion or struggles with setting healthy boundaries.

Working with the Empress means reflecting on how compassion has shaped your life. Has love been unconditional, or has it come with expectations? Have you struggled with self-nurturing, or do you give to others without replenishing yourself? Understanding this relationship with compassion is key to moving toward emotional wholeness.

FERTILITY
NURTURING
GROWTH
ABUNDANCE
MOTHER FIGURE
MOTHER NATURE
TENDERNESS
RECEIVING LAVISH REWARDS
EXPERIENCING LUXURY

VIBRANT HEALTH
EMBRACING THE NATURAL
LIFE GIVING

ADDITIONAL ASSOCIATIONS
CRYSTAL   - EMERALD
ASTROLOGY   - VENUS
ELEMENT   - EARTH
NUMEROLOGY - THREE

The Empress - meaning & associations

The Emperor – The Art of Discipline

The Emperor represents structure, stability and authority. He is the guiding force that instills order, responsibility and personal power. Where the Empress nurtures growth, the Emperor provides the foundation that makes growth sustainable.

The Emperor exists both externally - as the father figure, societal rules, laws and expectations - and internally, as the ability to create structure in your own life. His lessons revolve around self-discipline, leadership and taking charge of your own direction.

Balanced discipline creates security and confidence, fostering strong decision-making, perseverance and self-mastery. However, if discipline was modeled through control or punishment, it can lead to fear of authority, resistance to structure or an excessive need for control. Examining this relationship helps determine whether discipline is a tool of empowerment or a source of struggle.

The Emperor reminds you that life does not simply unfold - you must engage with it, shape it and take responsibility for your direction. Understanding discipline in a healthy way brings clarity and focus, making it easier to take action and stay true to your path.

AUTHORITY
LEADERSHIP
ACHIEVEMENT
RISING TO POSITIONS OF POWER
ACCOMPLISHMENT
FATHER FIGURE
BEING JUST AND FAIR
TAKING CHARGE
PROTECTOR OR DEFENDER

STRUCTURE & SECURITY
ESTABLISHING LAW & ORDER
CONFIDENCE

ADDITIONAL ASSOCIATIONS
CRYSTAL   - CARNELIAN
ASTROLOGY   - ARIES
ELEMENT   - FIRE
NUMEROLOGY - FOUR

The Emperor - meaning & associations

The Hierophant – Inherited Community

The Hierophant represents tradition, inherited beliefs and the collective systems that shape how the world is understood. He embodies the structure of religion, culture, education and societal expectations.

From an early age, conditioning instills certain rules, customs and ideologies. Some provide valuable guidance, while others create limitations or even lasting wounds. The Hierophant challenges you to examine which inherited beliefs align with your true self and which have been accepted without question.

As a teacher and guide, the Hierophant offers knowledge and wisdom, but his role is not to dictate your path - only to provide a foundation from which to explore your own truth. Many struggle with this energy when feeling trapped by rigid expectations or belief systems. The key to working with the Hierophant is discernment - learning to take what serves you and release what does not.

He also tests the ability to remain true to oneself while engaging with the larger world. Can you stand firm in your own beliefs without becoming rigid or closed off? Can you interact with tradition while still allowing space for personal evolution? The balance between individuality and collective influence is a vital part of the journey.

Through the Empress, the Emperor and the Hierophant, the foundation of identity becomes clearer. Understanding pre-conditioning allows for conscious self-creation, rather than simply existing as a product of external influences.

Shedding these layers is not about rejecting everything learned but about reclaiming the power to choose. It is the process of recognizing where conditioning has limited growth and stepping into a more authentic way of being. This stage of the journey is not always easy, but it is essential - the work of peeling away the unessential so the true self can emerge.

TRADITIONS	SEEKING GUIDANCE
BEING ORTHODOX	SPIRITUAL ADVISORS
KINDNESS	KNOWING YOUR FAITH
DIVINE LAW	
CONFORMITY	**ADDITIONAL ASSOCIATIONS**
CULTURAL HERITAGE	CRYSTAL - DIAMOND
RITUAL & CEREMONY	ASTROLOGY - TAURUS
ADOPTING TO THE SYSTEM	ELEMENT - EARTH
BEING PART OF A GROUP	NUMEROLOGY - FIVE

The Heirophant - meaning & associations

Knowledge of the Self

Here, you begin to establish who you are - for yourself. This stage is where you define, explore and master the self. It is essential preparation for the lessons ahead. Defining individuality requires awareness of pre-conditioning, ensuring that the self being established is authentic. This is where morals, ethics and core identity take shape.

Once the self is defined, the process shifts to testing, refining and mastering something that will be repeated many times along the journey. Understanding patterns and behaviors is key. It allows for the conscious preservation of what truly is while building the strength to strip away what is not.

Around the pre-teen years, a person naturally begins to define themselves, forming individual values and beliefs. This stage is represented by the Lovers card. On a spiritual path, this process happens again and again. Each time, there is an opportunity to refine, to deepen understanding, to integrate past lessons. The goal is not perfection - perfection is unattainable. The goal is simply to be better, to grow and evolve with each iteration.

Once the self has been (re)established, the journey moves outward, facing the tests of the world. These tests come in many forms, often revealing how firmly rooted one is in self-awareness. A simple example is someone overstepping a boundary - how you respond speaks volumes about where you stand in your knowledge of self.

Strength represents just that - strength. True fortitude is the ability to stand in the face of adversity and remain aligned with your core self. This is the essence of the Strength card. Strength on the spiritual path is not about imposing your identity onto others. It is not forceful. It does not demand. True strength is simply being - unwavering in authenticity, regardless of external circumstances.

The Lovers – For the Love of Morals

The Lovers marks the moment of stepping into personal belief, identity and choice. The Hierophant has provided all he can - now the question is, where to from here? This is the stage of consciously deciding who you are, what you believe in and what guides your moral and ethical compass. As these foundations take shape, they naturally influence the types of partnerships and connections you are drawn to.

As relationships evolve, so do the decisions made within them. We are never static - constantly shifting, learning and refining ourselves. The Lovers is the true representation of love, relationships and passion, but beyond that, it is about the establishment of the self. It speaks to the development of personal values, beliefs and ethics, as well as the connection both to oneself and to others.

The Hierophant presented the framework, offering the options of who one *could* be, but the Lovers is the act of *choosing* who to become. At its core, this card represents free will - the ability to define beliefs, morals and ethics on one's own terms. It asks, "Have you allowed society to mold you into its image? Have you accepted its definitions of right and wrong without question? Or have you examined these structures and found that they do not align with your truth?"

The Lovers is not about blind acceptance, nor is it about rejection for the sake of rebellion. It is about discernment - choosing what resonates and consciously shaping an authentic path forward..

RELATIONSHIPS NEW & OLD
DECISIONS & CHOICES
LOVE, TRUST, PASSION & DESIRE
COMPLETENESS OR WHOLENESS
SEXUALITY & INTIMACY
VALUES & PERSONAL BELIEFS
MARRIAGE OR UNION
CONNECTION WITH OTHERS
BEING TRUE TO YOURSELF

KNOW YOUR STANDARDS
CORE MORALS
CREATING A BELIEF SYSTEM

ADDITIONAL ASSOCIATIONS
CRYSTAL   - RUBY
ASTROLOGY   - GEMINI
ELEMENT   - AIR
NUMEROLOGY - SIX

The Lovers - meaning & associations

The Chariot — A Disciplined Ego

As we grow and shape ourselves into who we choose to be, we begin to master the self. Through discipline, self-awareness and inner control, we come to understand that willpower allows us to overcome any obstacle. The Chariot marks this stage of victory - the rewards of self-mastery are deeply fulfilling.

The Charioteer holds no reins, for control is no longer external. He has reached a level where sheer will, and determination guide his path. The dual beings pulling the Chariot remind us that mastery is not just about light, but also about integrating the shadow. True triumph comes from balancing both aspects of the self. Having reached this point, the Charioteer is ready to leave behind the familiar and venture forward, testing the full extent of his mastery.

The Chariot exudes confidence, determination and self-assertion. It calls for focus, urging the alignment of intention and action. This is the moment to rise above obstacles and distractions, to channel energy with precision. Now that beliefs, morals and ethics have been consciously chosen, the task is to master personal power. Whether following society's path or forging an entirely different one, the challenge remains the same - owning that choice and walking it with conviction.

The Chariot is the mastery of ego - not in arrogance, but in self-assured pride. It is the process of merging and balancing all aspects of the self, integrating what has been learned and stepping forward with unwavering purpose.

CONFIDENCE	ASSUMING AUTHORITY
WILL POWER	KNOWING WHO YOU ARE
TEST OF SKILLS	HEALTHY EGO
TRAVEL OR JOURNEY	
DETERMINED TO SUCCEED	**ADDITIONAL ASSOCIATIONS**
FOCUSING YOUR INTENT	CRYSTAL - PYRITE
MASTERING EMOTIONS	ASTROLOGY - CANCER
DISCIPLINE	ELEMENT - WATER
SELF-MASTERY	NUMEROLOGY - SEVEN

The Chariot - meaning & associations

Strength – The Gentleness Within

Having mastered the self, the next challenge is to be tested on this newfound strength. The real question is - do we truly understand what strength is? Is it about power and dominance, or is it strength of character? The answer within the Strength card is simple - it is the quiet, gentle strength that comes from within. It is compassion for oneself and for others.

As the journey continues, there will be tests that push patience, resilience and the very core of who we have become. These challenges will not be overcome through force or resistance but through understanding, patience and inner stamina. True strength is not about fighting against obstacles but about meeting them with grace. It is the ability to remain centered, to respond rather than react, to allow compassion and understanding to guide the way.

Strength is often associated with physical power, but the Strength card teaches of a force far greater - the ability to stand firm in who you are without aggression. Mastery of the self and the ego brings the ability to be assertive without being forceful, to take pride in who you are without arrogance. Strength is not about imposing your will on others but about allowing them to witness the steadiness of your presence and take from it whatever they need. True strength does not demand - it simply is.

INNER STRENGTH
COURAGE
GENTLE APPROACH
SOFT CONTROL
GALLANT SPIRIT
STAMINA & ENDURANCE
UNDERSTANDING OF OTHERS (EMPATHY)
INDIRECTLY GUIDING
PERSEVERANCE

RELIABLE
STRENGTH OF CHARACTOR

ADDITIONAL ASSOCIATIONS
CRYSTAL   - TIGER IRON
ASTROLOGY - LEO
ELEMENT   - FIRE
NUMEROLOGY - EIGHT

Strength - meaning & associations

Lessons

At this stage, there is a deeper understanding of the self - the ability to distinguish between the core self and external influences. Now, the true test begins. Moving into the lessons, you will discover just how strong you truly are.

Some lessons may be faced only once, while others may return again and again. This depends on how much work has been done in earlier stages, particularly in confronting pre-conditioning. These lessons reveal the deeper truths of the self, peeling back layers to expose both light and shadow. Through them, peace, intuition and enlightenment begin to take root. These lessons are not meant to be rushed - there is no final destination, only raw understanding.

The lessons of trust, faith, shadow, death and true spirituality unfold here. Whether these lessons break you or build you is a choice. With all the knowledge and awareness gained so far, working through them becomes simpler - not easier, but clearer. Everyone will encounter these experiences in some form, but how they unfold is unique to each individual. This is where paths begin to diverge.

The first lesson is the Hermit, the lesson of spirituality. Spiritual awareness often begins with a single moment of realization light switched on, illuminating the path. This is the Hermit's lantern, and it is all that is needed. Spirituality does not require seeing the entire road ahead, only the next step. Trying to look too far forward only creates distortions and unnecessary fear. The lesson of the Hermit is to trust in the present and allow the path to unfold.

The lesson of change is taught by the Wheel of Fortune. The wheel turns regardless of resistance - whether you choose to move with it or be flattened beneath it is entirely up to you. Life moves through cycles, shifts and transitions, and these should not be feared. While change is often met with resistance, it is, more often than not, a beautiful and necessary experience. Change is part of why we are here - it is woven into the very nature of existence.

Justice teaches the lesson of morality. This is where the concept of right and wrong is explored in relation to personal beliefs. It ties back to the Lovers, where choices were made about identity, ethics and values. Justice reminds us that morality must remain in balance to be truly fair and just.

Prudence, represented by the Hanged Man, connects with this lesson. Knowing what is right is not just about principles - it is about discernment. Not every battle is yours to fight, not every offering is yours to make. The Tarot beautifully illustrates the four cardinal virtues, which play a central role in self-awareness:

- Fortitude – Strength
- Morality – Justice
- Prudence – Hanged Man
- Temperance – Temperance

Letting go is one of the hardest lessons to learn. Many struggle with it because they do not know how or are simply afraid. Yet, the art of letting go is one of the most rewarding skills. Shedding unnecessary burdens lightens the load, allowing space for new growth. Grief often accompanies this process, and that is natural. Mourning is not a sign of weakness but of strength.

Through letting go, the lesson of balance emerges. True peace comes from balance, but there is always the risk of becoming lost in it. Spirituality must be integrated into daily life, not used as an escape. Keeping one foot on the ground is essential - this journey is about living fully, not drifting away from reality.

With balance in place, it becomes possible to face the lesson of the Devil - the shadow self. This is where deep personal work happens. Shadow work is neither easy nor comfortable, but it is necessary. The key is maintaining balance and practicing compassion-based honesty. Shadow work is not about tearing yourself apart; it is about deeper understanding.

Many facilitators offer powerful workshops on working with the shadow self, and these experiences can be invaluable. If this process feels overwhelming, seeking guidance can make it gentler. This is some of the most transformative work you can do for yourself - difficult but profoundly rewarding.

The Tower brings the experience of transformation. If you have been through it before, you know how disruptive it can be. It is chaos and destruction, but for a reason - true transformation is not meant to be easy. If it were, everyone would do it. Yet, as painful as the process may be, emerging on the other side feels like stepping into something new, something clearer.

Looking back at past experiences of transformation, consider how the next one can be navigated with greater awareness. Each cycle holds wisdom, and using past lessons without judgment or emotional attachment allows for authentic understanding. Transformation is not about clinging to what was but embracing what is becoming.

The Hermit – The Introspective Tutor

The Hermit can be described as a journey within a Journey. After facing many of life's challenges we are inclined to begin questioning, questions that ask "why" and "what for"? We find ourselves at the start of a path that is walked mostly alone, with only a few encounters with beings of pure wisdom that guide and direct us further down this path. The journey within is one of stepping away from the outside world to step inside the self and have a deeper look at who we are, and why we are. By transcending as we have along our journey so far, we have become wise enough to know that there is deeper meaning to this life. The deeper meaning sits within us and beckons us to delve deep within and truly understand the Soul.

A journey within oneself has great importance. The Hermit understands that the answers he seeks will only come from within and through quiet introspection. The Hermit is about stepping within oneself to gain a better perspective. There have been and will be times where we need to step out of society and the day-to-day hum drum to either reassess or to better understand a situation or even ourselves. To learn from a deeper perspective, one needs a quiet place to sit and contemplate. This is the nature of The Hermit. When dealing with The Hermit though, one must remember not to get too caught up in the solitude; and that once the search is done and the answers have been received, we need to step back into the world again to carry on with our path.

INNER KNOWLEDGE	PERSONAL QUEST
SPIRITUAL WISDOM	BEING A TEACHER OR GUIDE
QUIET INTROSPECTION	SEEKING SOLITUDE
PLANNING & STRATEGISING	
SPIRITUAL INSIGHT	**ADDITIONAL ASSOCIATIONS**
WISE COUNSEL	CRYSTAL - PERIDOT
LOOKING WITHIN FOR ANSWERS	ASTROLOGY - VIRGO
SEARCH FOR DEEPER MEANING	ELEMENT - EARTH
GIVING OR RECEIVING GUIDANCE	NUMEROLOGY - NINE

The Hermit - meaning & associations

The Wheel — The Karmic Cycle

When one is standing on the inside looking out, their view of the world is whole. One can see how everything is connected, and they understand that the Wheel will turn and weave as it must, that every turn has a purpose. Being able to see and understand that we are all connected, opens our consciousness to a new level of understanding. We no longer need to ask "why" or "what for". We instead simply acknowledge the process of life. The Wheel teaches the lesson of Universal Order. To understand it is to know that the path it weaves for us is the path we have weaved for ourselves. We create our own destiny, and we do this daily with our thoughts, decisions and actions. Our ability to take responsibility for these, coupled with our understanding that not all is in our control, will shift us into a new perspective.

The wheel of life will always turn regardless of our thoughts and actions. In the journey through life, we continually experience the end of one phase and the start of another. The wheel of life doesn't acknowledge stagnation. The Wheel is about acknowledging and accepting this fact. Once we can accept this, our lives become much simpler as we learn that we can only control certain things and that it is unnecessary to stress about the things we have no control over, rather focusing our energy into what we do have control over.

TURNING POINT
TURN OF EVENTS
ADVANCEMENT
DESTINY
WITNESSING LIFE'S PROCESSES
MIRACLES
CHANGE IN FORTUNE
DISCOVERING YOUR PURPOSE
ALTERING YOUR PRESENT COURSE

SEE HOW THINGS ARE CONNECTED
SEEING THE BIGGER PICTURE
CHANGE IN PERSPECTIVE

ADDITIONAL ASSOCIATIONS
CRYSTAL   - JADE
ASTROLOGY   - JUPITOR
ELEMENT   - FIRE
NUMEROLOGY - ONE & ZERO

The Wheel - meaning & associations

Justice – Universal Laws

Lady Justice ensures that we receive the karma we have earned. This is a time to take full responsibility for the life lived so far, acknowledging the cause and effect of every thought, action and choice. Justice reminds us that we are accountable only for ourselves - our words, our integrity and the energy we put into the world. The actions of others are not ours to judge or control, nor should they shape who we are at our core.

With awareness comes the need for reflection. Having gained insight into the impact of our choices, we must decide how to move forward. Justice calls for conscious decision-making. Do we continue on the path of enlightenment, taking full ownership of our reality, or do we retreat into ignorance, avoiding the weight of self-awareness?

Justice is not just a concept of fairness - it is the universal force that ensures balance, deeply aligned with the Hermetic Principles. The principle of mentalism reminds us that all is mind; our reality begins with thought. Correspondence teaches that what exists within us is reflected externally.

Vibration reminds us that karma moves through shifting energies, returning consequences in accordance with what we have put into motion. Polarity and rhythm show that balance is a natural process - justice exists because imbalance exists, and all things move in cycles, including karmic resolution.

Cause and effect is the heart of Justice, reinforcing that nothing happens by chance. The principle of gender reminds us that true justice requires both decisive action and intuitive discernment, represented by the sword and scales.

Justice is not about reward or punishment - it is the natural law of cause and consequence. By aligning with these truths, we gain clarity in navigating life. With this understanding, we no longer see life as fair or unfair but as the unfolding of choices and their outcomes. Justice teaches us to accept what it is, to take responsibility for what we create and to move forward with awareness and integrity.

FAIRNESS	RECOGNISING KARMA
EQUALITY	JUSTICE WILL BE SERVED
BEING ETHICAL	SEEING ALL SIDES TO A STORY
DOING WHAT IS RIGHT	
TAKING RESPONSIBILITY	**ADDITIONAL ASSOCIATIONS**
ACKNOWLEDGING THE TRUTH	CRYSTAL - PETRIFIED WOOD
DETERMINING THE RIGHT ACTION	ASTROLOGY - LIBRA
DECISIONS WITH ALL FACTS IN MIND	ELEMENT - AIR
UNDERSTANDING CAUSE & EFFECT	NUMEROLOGY - TWO

Justice - meaning & associations

Hanged Man – The Cost of Sacrifice

As the journey continues, sacrifices must be made to grow further. These are not always small, and they often exist within the material world. To move toward enlightenment, attachment to the physical must loosen, allowing the soul to take the lead. The lessons of Justice have prepared us for this stage, making it clear that sacrifice is not about loss but about creating space for something greater.

The Hanged Man teaches that true understanding comes not from control, but from surrender. This is the moment where resistance must cease, and instead, trust must take its place. The old ways of seeing the world no longer serve, and so a shift in perspective is required. This is not an action of force but of acceptance - allowing oneself to be suspended in uncertainty, to sit in stillness and let wisdom emerge.

In this space of suspension, time itself feels different. What once seemed urgent fades into insignificance, and what was overlooked now becomes clear. The mind slows, the ego quiets, and a deeper knowing begins to surface. This is where the soul takes precedence, no longer dictated by human limitations but instead guiding from a place of higher awareness.

The Hanged Man asks for trust. It is a difficult lesson because it requires release - release of control, of certainty, of old attachments. But in this release, something incredible happens. The soul aligns with something greater, moving beyond the need for external validation or material security. What was once sacrificed is revealed to be an illusion, and what remains is truth.

This is not a punishment but a necessary initiation. Growth requires letting go, and the Hanged Man teaches how to surrender to this process with grace. The path ahead will demand more of the self, and this moment of stillness is preparation. It is here that the greatest insights arise, not through struggle, but through the willingness to simply be, to see and to trust in what comes next.

CHANGE IN ONES PERSPECTIVE
SPIRITUAL AWARENESS
A NEW LEVEL OF CONSCIOUSNESS
GIVING UP CONTROL
LETTING GO
ACCEPTING LIFE'S PROCESSES
COMPLETE TURN AROUND
CHANGE IN OLD PRIORITIES
MAKING SACRIFICES

PUTTING SELF INTEREST ASIDE
LIVING IN THE MOMENT
CHANGING FOR THE GREATER GOOD

ADDITIONAL ASSOCIATIONS
CRYSTAL   - MOSS AGATE
ASTROLOGY   - NEPTUNE
ELEMENT   - WATER
NUMEROLOGY   - THREE

The Hanged Man - meaning & associations

Death – Peace in Letting Go

To move forward - whether within this lifetime or into the next - we must experience death. This is not just physical death, but the continual shedding of what no longer serves us. Society has conditioned us to fear death, yet it is the one certainty in life. The irony is that death is not an end but a transformation, a release of the unessential so that we may move forward unburdened.

The lessons of Death are not about loss, but renewal. In life, we face countless metaphorical deaths - relationships end, beliefs evolve, identities shift. Each death clears space for something new. Holding on to what has outlived its purpose only creates stagnation. The Death card reminds us that clinging to the past prevents growth, while surrendering to change allows for true evolution.

No one escapes death, and yet it is not to be feared. Just as the seasons change and nature cycles through birth, decay and rebirth, so too must we. Old thoughts, attachments and perceptions must die so that we may step into something new. Death is not destruction - it is transition. It is the doorway to the next stage of the journey, a necessary passage that ensures we continue forward with clarity and purpose.

NECESSARY CHANGE	CHANGE IN STATUS
DYING OFF OF THE OLD	MOVING INTO THE UNKNOWN
CUTTING OUT WHATS NOY REQUIRED	CLEARING OUT THE EXCESS
TRANSFORMATION OR TRANSITIONING	
CLOSE OF A CHAPTER	**ADDITIONAL ASSOCIATIONS**
LETTING GO OF THE PAST	CRYSTAL - OBSIDIAN
FOCUSING ON THE ESSENTIALS	ASTROLOGY - SCORPIO
INESCAPABLE CHANGE	ELEMENT - WATER
CHANGE IN OLD ATTITUDES	NUMEROLOGY - FOUR

Death - meaning & associations

Temperance — The Tempered Soul

With the right blend of elements, balance is found - this is Temperance. True balance comes from having everything in the correct measure, taking only what is needed and leaving the rest behind. It is also the reminder not to fear taking what is necessary. Temperance is the harmony between necessity and desire, ensuring that neither excess nor deprivation takes hold. This equilibrium comes from within - no external force can create it.

Since choosing to walk this path, life has felt like a constant swing between extremes, a rollercoaster of lessons and experiences. Only after learning the lessons of Death does true balance emerge. Temperance is the point of equilibrium, the place where peace is found. It teaches that overindulgence weighs us down, taking more than necessary becomes a burden, and taking too little leaves us unfulfilled.

Temperance is the mastery of balance, moderation and self-restraint. It is the right blend of ego, emotion and soul, reminding us to find the middle ground in all things. It is not about denying experience but about maintaining equilibrium. In the face of life's challenges, the ability to remain centered and focused allows for the steady, purposeful movement forward. Temperance is not a single moment of peace but the continuous act of maintaining it.

ACHIEVING HARMONY & BALANCE
MODERATION
AVOIDING EXCESS
SKILFUL MANAGEMENT
BLENDING OF OPPOSITES
REACH A COMPROMISE
FEELING CENTRED
FEELING OF WELL-BEING
RIGHT COMBINATION OF ELEMENTS

RECOVERY & HEALING
JOINING WITH OTHERS
BEING ABLE TO FLOURISH

ADDITIONAL ASSOCIATIONS
CRYSTAL   -KUNZITE
ASTROLOGY   - SAGITTARIUS
ELEMENT   - FIRE
NUMEROLOGY - FIVE

Temperance - meaning & associations

The Devil – The Shadow Within

Maintaining our true balance is challenged by the devil within us. Our shadow self, where inner ignorance and humanism still lurk beneath the surface, challenging us. Testing our Fool to the fullest. Have we truly removed our human bonds and progressed to that next level? Will we simply slip back into our material world and revel in the delights of the physical or will we maintain our soulful equilibrium and once and for all remove our bonds with the physical.

The Devil is representative of the lessons of addiction, love of the material, the seven deadly sins if you will. The Devil resides within us, he is not an outward force compelling you into a direction that you do not wish to go. The Devil is an aspect of the self and how we chose to deal with this Devil will assist in deciding our Path going forward.

It is Human nature to perceive the world as good or bad, whereas the reality is that good and bad cannot be separated, just as we cannot separate ourselves from our shadow. The Devil reminds us of our fears, in particular our fear of being Human and making Human errors. Fear is a natural part of who we are, it's a mechanism that warns us against life-or-death threats and situations. However, the fear of the irrational is a different story, irrational being something that isn't life threatening. We are more than capable of removing the bonds that irrational fears create as we have created these bonds for ourselves. For us to continue unhindered on our path it is necessary to remove these irrational fears.

BOUND BY FEAR
MATERIALISTIC
OBSESSION
ADDICTION
OVERINDULGENCE
FEELING TIED DOWN
BEING SUBMISSIVE TO ANOTHER
IGNORANCE
FEAR OF THE UNKNOWN

CHOOSING TO STAY IN THE DARK
ONLY SEEING THE WORST, DESPAIR

ADDITIONAL ASSOCIATIONS
CRYSTAL - TEKTITE
ASTROLOGY - CAPRICORN
ELEMENT - EARTH
NUMEROLOGY - SIX

The Devil - meaning & associations

The Tower − Building an Empire

To remove the last of our physical bonds we must break and destroy what we have built up. We need to once again start our lives with a clean slate for us to build our empire. We cannot have a simple Tower as our castle, we are worthy of great things, we haven't worked this hard to be rewarded with something so simple and small as the Tower. It is time to knock down that Tower and build us into who we must become, who our Soul yearns to be. We do, however, remain humble with the knowing that external, material things cannot bring us fulfilment. That the empire we are building is within us.

To free ourselves from the Devil within we must remove it completely, break it down until it is nothing. This will leave us with a clear foundation on which to build. This is a humbling experience. For us to become Emperors of our Empire, we must first learn to be humble so that we may rule as a true, honest and enlightened Soul.

At certain stages in life, we hit points of stagnation, where we seem to be just ambling through life. The Tower coming in currently is a clear indication that some serious change is required – whether we like it or not. As with Death, we need the necessary removal of certain possessions and aspects of the self that are no longer serving a need in our Life. If we can acknowledge that these things have been removed for a reason, and we can understand this reasoning, our journey becomes much simpler and easier to deal with. The Tower will usually happen when we ignore Death, or when we are fearful of letting the unnecessary aspects of ourselves go.

NECESSARY CHAOS OR DESTRUCTION
SUDDEN CHANGE
ENDING OF THE OLD AND UNNECESSARY
END OF A PHASE OF STAGNATION
DISRUPTED PLANS,
EXPERIENCING A CRISIS
EMOTIONAL OUTBURST
EXPLODING IN ANGER
BEING HUMBLED

BLOW TO THE EGO
SUDDENLY SEEING THE TRUTH
CRASHING DOWN AROUND YOU

ADDITIONAL ASSOCIATIONS

CRYSTAL   - LODESTONE
ASTROLOGY   - MARS
ELEMENT   - FIRE
NUMEROLOGY   - SEVEN

The Tower - meaning & associations

Attainments

Attainments are not goals! It is important to remember that one should not place goals on their spiritual path. When we have goals for our path, we lose sight of purpose and the point of the journey. Instead, our journey becomes one of stress, anxiety and disappointment. When we attach goals, we move from being present on our journey to a place of expectation and we find ourselves living in the future. Attainments are not found in the future, but rather within the present moment. It is only in the present that we can be at peace, listen to our intuition and experience enlightenment.

These attainments are found by working through the lessons, understanding and knowing our core authentic self, and shedding our pre-conditions, behaviours and masks. These attainments then become practices, which begin to shape you into your authenticity. These attainments are what make the spiritual journey one well worth taking. These are the things many search lifetimes to find.

When you have goals on your spiritual path, you create unnecessary stress for yourself. So do not look at these attainments as goals or something you need to work for. Also know that these attainments are already inside of you. They are not external-based aspects you are trying to incorporate into yourself. Our ability to achieve inner peace is far easier than we think Inner peace is a state of mind. It is mindful awareness of Self. We all certainly have intuition, even though we just may not always trust it. This is because you are not used to using it, but it becomes stronger with practice. Then Enlightenment, well you were enlightened to begin with, you just didn't see it at first.

The Star – Soft Wishes

When one is content and at peace, they are capable of achieving the impossible. For centuries, people have been looking to the stars for guidance and direction. The Star is a depiction of pure mindfulness - as it is in the state of being mindful that we can be fully aware, at peace and manifest our true desires. This is the nature of The Star. Maintaining this state of mindfulness and peace becomes a practice - and the more one practice, the more you are able to develop this natural aspect of yourself. Having the experience of dealing with our inner Devil and rooting it out, we are left with a sense of calm clarity. We know we can achieve anything and we step into our authentic self, no longer held by the bonds of being human.

The negativity, ignorance and despair of the past is gone and is replaced with a sense of wellbeing and completeness. Our Life Path seems simpler, and we are led to believe that we have reached the level of complete enlightenment; a moment of sheer bliss - those moments of pure contentment where all is well with the world. Life is easier and our Path is clear. The Star refers to those moments of clarity where we have a full understanding of everything we need to know. These moments usually come after a time of hardship, sorrow or suffering.

OPTIMISM, HOPE	SERENITY
WISHES COMING TRUE	FEELING CENTRED
BLESSINGS, HEALING	TRANQUIL HARMONY
ASPIRATIONS	**ADDITIONAL ASSOCIATIONS**
FAITH	
GAINING MOTIVATION	CRYSTAL - MOLDAVITE
SEEING YOUR INNER STRENGTH	ASTROLOGY - AQUARIUS
RECEIVING ANSWERS	ELEMENT - AIR
GIVING OR SHARING	NUMEROLOGY - EIGHT

The Star - meaning & associations

The Moon - Illusions

Living within this blissful sense of completion, we begin to once again become unaware that we are being led by our emotions and our human state once again. The Soul does not need to feel human emotions to know it is complete. The illusions created by the dreamy Moon have disguised our Soul's true direction and guidance. Being guided by the light of the Moon is not as it seems - our imaginations are left to run wild, and this can give rise to fears and anxieties. We become unsure if what we are seeing and feeling is real. The world of dreams is also the world of nightmares. We must not allow ourselves to get lost within the Sub-Conscious and allow our minds to run away with us, for what lies in the dark is uncertain, and uncertainty gives rise to fear.

It is for us to shed light on this darkness and see everything for what it really is.

When exploring the realms of the sub-conscious, be mindful not to get caught up in your imagination. The illusions created by the dreamy Moon can disguise one's true direction and guidance. As much as imagination is where we create our world, we must be aware of not losing our hold on true reality. Being guided by the light of the Moon, things are not always what they seem. Remember to keep shedding light on the darkness, so you are able see everything for what it real(ity)ly is.

Representing the fear of the unknown and the misunderstood, the Moon sheds a strange light on the world, causing us to struggle to call things as they are. Driven predominantly by our imaginations, the Moon can bring our biggest nightmares to life or make it seem as if our dreams have come true. The Moon state of mind is a strange place to be and can extend as far as our imaginations can go. We struggle to focus on what is reality and what is just our minds playing with us.

FEARS AND PHOBIAS
OVERCOME BY ANXIETIES
BEING UNREALISTIC
MISINTERPRETING THE TRUTH
DECEIT OR DECEIVING YOURSELF
CHASING A PIPE DREAM
HAVING VIVID OR REALISTIC DREAMS
HAVING NO DIRECTION
FEELING LOST OR BEWILDERED

CAUGHT UP IN ADDICTIONS
OVER ACTIVE IMAGINATION

ADDITIONAL ASSOCIATIONS

CRYSTAL - MOONSTONE
ASTROLOGY - MOON
ELEMENT - WATER
NUMEROLOGY - NINE

The Moon - meaning & associations

The Sun - Enlightenment

By shedding the Light of the Soul on the darkness that is our sub-conscious, everything becomes clear and we see our fears and anxieties for what they really are: just our imagination. We learn to trust the intuitive abilities of our sub-conscious and put fears and anxieties out of our mind. We allow our Soul to take charge once again and we learn to not only feel the blissfulness of the Star, but to understand it as well. The Sun is the Soul's guiding light. Enlightened and wise, the Sun guides the Fool to his revelation. Allowing him to see clearly the true nature of things; authentic reality.

It is time to be one with yourself, to embrace who you are and be carefree in this knowledge and allow it to just be. It is in this moment that one can know and understand their greatness. We can take on any challenge Life may hand us. We radiate our enlightenment and revel in its light.

The Sun is representative of the conscious mind, a place full of light and vitality. It's where we do our clear thinking and planning. The Sun in all its warmth and splendour is the epitome of confidence, glowing with pure enlightenment and unlimited energy. A sunny state of mind, the Sun card has an element of innocence to it and gives us a sense that everything from here on will be far easier to manage, we become carefree as the Fool once again. However, we have become far wiser than the Fool when he initially started out on his journey. It is with the knowledge he has gained that he can live in an innocent and carefree manner, but do not mistake this attitude for a foolish one, there is much wisdom and knowledge behind that carefree smile.

YOUTHFUL FEELING	OUTSHINING THE REST
FEELING ENERGISED	HAVING CONFIDENCE
EXPERIENCING ACCOMPLISHMENT	KNOWING YOUR WORTH
ENLIGHTENMENT	
NEW LEVEL OF INSIGHT	**ADDITIONAL ASSOCIATIONS**
MOMENT OF GLORY	CRYSTAL - AMBER
INTELLECTUAL BREAKTHROUGH	ASTROLOGY - SUN
FEELINGS OF VITALITY	ELEMENT - FIRE
FEELINGS OF FREEDOM	NUMEROLOGY - ONE

The Sun - meaning & associations

Revelation

To have revelation, it is important to have a sound understanding of what judgment means. On your journey, you will need to have sound judgment. You will be needing to make judgment calls, decisions and choices. This type of judgment does not consider the emotional perspective.

When you apply emotions to your judgments, choices and decisions, you lose the revelation. By judging and assessing without emotional triggers or attachments, you have true, authentic revelations. This is where your lessons become practices. This is core enlightenment. It is utilizing rational judgment. It is where you need to understand your triggers, lessons and pre-conditioning, so that when seeking revelation, you are seeking from an authentic standpoint.

Throughout this book, I have mentioned working from a place of no judgment. This is because it is one of the skills needed to have Authentic awareness. Judgment should never be emotion-based. When you bring emotion into making a judgment (or decision), you are reacting from behaviors and patterns; not your authentic self. Keep your judgment honest, gentle, and detached from emotions.

Judgement – Day of Atonement

We will all eventually have our Judgment Day where we will be held accountable for our thoughts and actions. This is where revelations happen. Judgment in this case doesn't include us being reprimanded or congratulated, rather it is our chance to acknowledge and understand the implications of our decisions. When it comes to the Judgment card, we are looking at a different type of Judgment altogether. It involves looking back and assessing. Then taking from these assessments the lessons that were learned along the way. It's a form of reflection where we can understand better and likely find gratitude. This form of judgment is a healing and enlightening experience, when done from an observational viewpoint and with the intention to simply understand.

In reaching our true Enlightenment, we can face our Judgment Day from a place of peace, tranquillity and pure understanding. We have removed the bonds of our human form and have allowed our Souls to shine through and radiate. Our Soul has called upon us to rise and face our true Judgment; it is time to reflect on the Path we have walked. In knowing all that is and understanding Life in it's true form, we understand that our judgment day does not consist of right or wrong, good or evil, but rather recognizing the Life we have lived and how we have grown from that experience. We have finally come to understand our true purpose of being here and having the experiences we have had. We are now ready for completion.

When it comes to the word 'judgement', we instantly associate it with the idea of what have you done and why have you done it. However, when it comes to the Judgement card, we are looking at a different type of Judgement altogether. It involves looking back, assessing and taking from these assessments the lessons that were learnt along the way. It's a form of reflection where we don't bring ourselves down for what we have or haven't done, but where we can reflect on what we can take away from what we have or haven't done. This form of judgement can be a very healing and enlightening experience.

END OF A PHASE OR FRESH START
AWAKENING,
HAVING A REVELATION
EFFORTS BEING REWARDED
MAKING DEFINITE DECISIONS
MAKING A STAND
DAY OF RECKONING
TRANSFORMATION
RENEWED HOPE

ABSOLUTION
UNBURDENING YOURSELF
RELEASING OF GUILT

ADDITIONAL ASSOCIATIONS
CRYSTAL   - AMETHYST
ASTROLOGY   - PLUTO
ELEMENT   - FIRE
NUMEROLOGY - TWO

Judgement - meaning & associations

Mastery

This is where you have mastered your path and where you will continue to master your path. This is the point, however, where we understand that the journey we have explored, can also begin here. The ego believes that it is whole and complete; or that the things outside of it complete who you are. You believe that you have mastered yourself and are master of yourself.

Then you have a Revelation and realize (real eyes) that you have not mastered yourself and are only just beginning. This is where your intuition and enlightenment come into play, and you understand that you have much learn. Here you begin to see your lessons and pre-conditions, as well as how these are impacting and shaping you. This is where you see yourself. This is the beauty of the journey: it flows both ways, has no beginning or end, and you realise that this is what makes it a complete cycle. Mastery is our endpoint in the Major Arcana, but it is not the endpoint of the journey. You will continue to master yourself throughout your lifetime. This is your purpose; this is part of why you exist. Come back to mastery as often as you need to. Each time you come back more humble, grateful, and loving.

The World – A Cycle Complete

This card represents that sense of completeness that we all experience at various stages through-out our lives. It's that feeling of having the entire World in your hands; that feeling of sheer contentment when everything is as it should be, and the World feels whole.

This happens when we know we have come full circle in a cycle and that for the present moment, all is well and we are content to live in the now; not worrying about our 'mistakes' of the past or stressing about what tomorrow might hold. All that matters is here and now, and we are comfortable in our completion; yet also aware that we have much still to learn and master.

We are now complete; we have endured Life's challenges and we have grown to become a Soul complete. We have reached our full Enlightenment and are able to venture once again out into the World with a knowing of who we are and what our purpose is. A journey that seemed trivial and foolish was worth stepping off the proverbial cliff for. We will soon be ready to commence with a new journey, finding ourselves back at the edge of the cliff, deciding whether or not to plunge into the journey ahead to see where it leads, or to remain where we are as the Fool.

COMPLETION, WHOLENESS
FEELING OF FULFILMENT
PERFECTION, SATISFACTION
CONTENTMENT
THE END RESULT
REALISING YOUR GOALS
ACHIEVING YOUR HEART'S DESIRE
FINDING THE PERFECT SOLUTION
FEELING ENGAGED WITH LIFE

HAVING PEACE OF MIND
COUNT YOUR BLESSINGS
ENJOYING LIFE'S PLEASURES

ADDITIONAL ASSOCIATIONS
CRYSTAL   - TURQUOISE
ASTROLOGY   - SATURN
ELEMENT   - EARTH
NUMEROLOGY   - THREE

The World - meaning & associations

Chapter 10

The Minor Arcana

The Minor Arcana is an expansion of the Major Arcana, and it sheds light on the day-to-day happenings of our lives. When reading Tarot, one should keep this in mind and consider the sub journey that is the Minor Arcana, utilizing it to see the full picture of any situation.

When we come into this lifetime, we are given the four basic tools we need in order to live fully, learn and make progress in our lives. The Minor Arcana breaks down these four tools into the lessons we need to learn to better utilize these elements or tools to our advantage.

The Minor Arcana as we know, consists of four suits which represent the four elements and the four core aspects of the self. We need to journey through these aspects so that we can gain a greater understanding of who, what and why we are. The journey through each suit is similar in that the core lessons are the same, however, these lessons become applicable to the relevant Suit's aspect. For example, Wands would have the same core lessons or journey as Pentacles, but would be focused on the energetic or creative aspects of the self and Pentacles would be focused on the material and physical aspects.

The Minor Arcana is a guide for the sub journeys in life - the journeys we take to embrace and master the aspects of the self. Work with the suit that relates to the aspect you are looking into. The journey for each suit is essentially the same. The difference is the aspect it relates to. There are additional associations that are worth taking into consideration as well, such as the numerology, astrology and element associations. These can add excellent insights into your readings.

Utilize the Minors to better and improve yourself. Consciously work through each suit. See and understand the progression and find how it relates to your path. Knowing where you are and what you have achieved is highly beneficial.

PHYSICAL ASPECT | EARTH BASED
Pentacles represents the physical aspects of our lives and are associated with the Earth element. Pentacles can help shed light on the following areas;

BODY	FAMILY
CAREER	SECURITY
HEALTH	FINANCES
HOME	POSSESSIONS

EMOTIONAL ASPECT | WATER BASED
Cups represent the emotional and intuitive aspects of our lives and are associated with the Water element. Cups can help shed light on the following areas;

FEELINGS	FRIENDSHIPS
CONNECTION	HEART MATTERS
INTUITION	EMOTIONAL STATE
RELATIONSHIPS	RELATABILITY

ENERGETIC ASPECT | FIRE BASED
Wands represent the creative and energetic aspects of our lives and are associated with the Fire element. Wands can help shed light on the following areas;

PASSION	CREATIVITY
CHANGE	ENERGY
BELIEFS	TRAVEL
MOVEMENT	IMAGINATION

MENTAL ASPECT | AIR BASED
Swords represents the mental aspects of our lives and are associated with the Air element. Swords can help shed light on the following areas;

INTELLECT	MIND STATE
LEARNING	ETHICS
REASONING	MORALS
STUDYING	CORE VALUES

Journey Through the Suits

ACES	OPPORTUNITY
TWOS	BALANCE
THREES	PLANNING
FOURS	FOUNDATION
FIVES	TESTS
SIXES	RESULTS
SEVENS	REVIEW
EIGHTS	ACTION
NINES	CONSEQUENCES
TENS	COMPLETION

Aces

Aces are the start of a new cycle or experience. They are filled with positivity and endless possibilities. They enter our lives to start us on a sub journey to learn and fully understand the lessons of its relevant Suit.

PENTACLES - The Ace of Pentacles symbolizes those moments when opportunities to master the material aspect of the self are given. Our lesson in the material starts here, how we progress and use those opportunities is key to us mastering this aspect of the self. The material aspect doesn't just refer to money or finances, but to all the physical aspects of our selves i.e. our health, our home, our physical possessions and our family. The opportunity for abundance, prosperity and building a stable foundation and trust has arrived. It's an indication that one needs to become real about their goals and turn their dreams into a reality.

MATERIAL STABILITY	THE MEANS TO REACH GOALS
STABLE SITUATION	HAVING TOTAL SECURITY
CAREER OPPORTUNITIES	EFFORTS BEING REWARDED
BUSINESS OPPORTUNITIES	BEING PRACTICAL OR REALISTIC
ACHIEVING RESULTS	SUPPORT SYSTEM OR STRUCTURE
IMPROVING YOUR BODY OR HEALTH	COMMON-SENSE

Ace of Pentacles - meaning & associations

CUPS - Those warm, loving feelings of a new relationship or friendship... this is the Ace of Cups. Being open to new relationship opportunities makes us open to experiencing new emotions and feelings. By expanding on these new feelings, we become more in-tune with who we are, and we feel our intuitive ability increasing. New doors are being opened to you, and it is time to follow the direction of your heart and intuition. Lessons of love, matters of the heart and understanding our spiritual aspects are now at the forefront - embrace this sweet journey.

NEW RELATIONSHIPS	TRUST YOUR INTUITION
EMOTIONAL TIES	IN TUNE WITH YOURSELF
GROWTH IN RELATIONSHIPS	DEEPENED INTUITION
DEEPER COMMITMENTS	EXPERIENCING INTIMACY
IN TOUCH WITH FEELINGS	EXPRESS LOVE & AFFECTION
UNDERSTANDING EMPATHY	FORGIVE & FORGET

Ace of Cups - meaning & associations

WANDS - The feeling of new, charged up energy is the Ace of Wands. It's that moment when we feel greatly inspired and ready to take on the world. We feel as if we can create and do anything. The opportunity for adventure and excitement, to grow in your personal power and to have the courage to explore your creative side. It's time to see your potential and have the confidence to reach for your dreams. Take the risks and be rewarded by what you desire.

VIBRANT, CREATIVE ENERGY	CONFIDENCE
NEW VENTURE OR MOVE	TAKING ON A CHALLENGE
EXPANDING ON YOUR POTENTIAL	OPEN TO POSSIBILITIES
GROWING YOUR TALENTS	TAKING A STAND
BEING AN INSPIRATION	BEING TRUE TO YOUR BELIEFS
CONCEIVING SOLUTIONS, IDEAS	FACING FEARS & GOING FOR IT

Ace of Wands - meaning & associations

SWORDS - Opportunities to expand and grow the mind are being offered, we are in a position to stretch our minds and see where this takes us. We feel open minded and ready to absorb every last bit of information we can. Opportunities regarding the mind, studies, clarity, mental growth and reason are now being offered. The time for mental challenges and stretching your mind has arrived.

NEW IDEAS	GAINING A CLEAR UNDERSTANDING
NEW WAY OF THINKING	NEW MIND SET
OPPORTUNITY TO STUDY	STRENGTH TO OVERCOME
BEING OBJECTIVE	ACHIEVEMENTS
FACING PROBLEMS HEAD ON	A SITUATION BEING RESOLVED
RIGHTING WRONGS	APPLYING LOGIC & REASON

Ace of Swords - meaning & associations

Twos

Twos are about understanding, establishing or maintaining balance. We are handed an opportunity, and for us to make the most of that opportunity, we need to understand balance. Sometimes the lessons of Two can be in the form of Life throwing us off balance or pulling the carpet out from under us. These lessons are given so that we may learn what balance truly is and how to maintain it.

PENTACLES - Finding balance between work and family, maintaining a steady balance with our finances, and most importantly finding the correct balance between being overly materialistic or being apathetic and having complete disregard for our material possessions. A reminder that we are infinitely powerful and capable of juggling all of life's challenges. One must have faith and confidence within themselves to know they can overcome any hurdle.

COPING SKILLS,	COPING WITH CHANGES IN DIRECTION
MAINTAINING BALANCE	OPEN TO ALL POSSIBILITIES
FLEXIBILITY	MANAGING A TRICKY SITUATION
COVERING ALL ASPECTS	MAINTAINING A FLUID BALANCE
BEING ABLE TO ADAPT	OPEN TO NEW CHALLENGES
HANDLING CHALLENGES	

Two of Pentacles - meaning & associations

CUPS - Our first time really experiencing a close, intimate relationship is usually a moment that stays with us through-out our Lifetime. Learning to have another person in your life is key to opening new emotional channels for yourself. As much as we all have our own journeys within our lifetimes, we all at some stage or another share our path with someone else. The Two of Cups is a close companion of The Lovers card and represents the idea of union to its fullest.

NEW RELATIONSHIP	UNION
PARTNERSHIPS	RECOGNISING A BOND
BALANCE	ATTRACTION
HARMONY	HEALING IN A RELATIONSHIP
MAKING A CONNECTION	MUTUAL AGREEMENT
BRINGING TOGETHER OPPOSITES	POSITIVE RESPONSE

Two of Cups - meaning & associations

WANDS - Being such an energetic Suit, the Two of Wands is about having the correct balance of power. The Two of Wands reminds us that we are infinitely powerful and capable of being 'kings', but we mustn't allow this power to control us. Take the gift of Divine, Universal power and mould it to work for you. Utilising your personal power to achieve greater good will bring you true rewards, but one must be wary of trying to dominate or control this power.

- SELF DISCIPLINE
- HAVING THE WORLD IN YOUR HANDS
- PERSONAL POWER
- BEING IN A POSITION OF AUTHORITY
- ACHIEVING YOUR GOALS
- TAKING A RISK, FACING FEARS HEAD-ON
- SPEAKING YOUR MIND
- SEIZE THE DAY
- INVENTING, PIONEERING
- DIFFERENT APPROACH
- DIVERTING FROM THE CROWD

Two of Wands - meaning & associations

SWORDS - The mind can be a very challenging place and overcoming fear that is holding us back can be even more challenging. However, if we look at the situation in retrospect and with a sensible rationale, we find that dealing with something such as fear is relatively simple and requires a good balanced mind that we are in control of. Avoiding our feelings and emotions, putting up a blockade to prevent anything from getting in or out... this is the Two of Swords - a depiction of true fear of our emotional state and avoiding what we know to be the truth.

- NOT DEALING WITH THE PRESENT
- AVOIDING ISSUES OR PROBLEMS
- DENYING REAL FEELINGS
- REFUSING THE FACTS
- BLINDED BY FEAR
- NEED TO FACE EMOTIONS
- AFRAID TO ACT
- BEING STUCK IN A RUT
- REFUSAL TO MAKE DECISIONS
- AVOIDANCE
- HIDING DISTRESS

Two of Swords - meaning & associations

Threes

Once we have learnt to fully understand balance and have achieved it, we can move onto the lesson of the Threes; which is a chance to restructure our Lives so that we can continue to maintain our balance. It is also a chance for celebrating our achievements in the Twos, a chance to stop and 'pat ourselves on the back'.

PENTACLES - Having found our physical balance, we can do some restructuring where we can see what is working and what isn't, to formulate a plan going forward. At certain stages, we require the help of others to achieve goals. Teamwork is necessary to progress forward and a team that can strategize and brainstorm together and implement what is needed will progress successfully.

MAKING GOOD PROGRESS	BEING PREPARED
CREATING OPPORTUNITIES	GETTING THE JOB DONE
COORDINATING WITH OTHERS	ACHIEVING GOALS
TEAM WORK	OVER ACHIEVING
PLANNING	KNOWING WHAT IS REQUIRED
STRATEGISING	HAVING NECESSARY RESOURCES

Three of Pentacles - meaning & associations

CUPS - Once we have experienced and fully understood an intimate relationship, we are able to expand on this and welcome more people into our Life. We learn about the fun emotions that we can experience such as joy, excitement and those other beautiful emotions that come from fulfilling friendships. As we learn from the Two of Cups that we all travel our paths with others as well as alone, the Three of Cups reinforces this idea, but from a group, friendship and community perspective. After all, who wants to experience all the good and exciting stuff alone?

CAUSE FOR CELEBRATION	SUPPORT GROUP
HIGH SPIRITS	COMPANIONSHIP
FULL OF ENERGY	UNITY WITH OTHERS
FRIENDSHIPS	COLLECTIVE CONSCIOUSNESS
VALUE IN COMMUNITY	CONNECTEDNESS OF THINGS
PART OF A TEAM	WEB OF LIFE

Three of Cups - meaning & associations

WANDS - Having mastered the balancing act of the Two, we can look around to see our options and gain a good perspective on where we would like to head with all this energy. It's time to take a step back and review the situation. A change in perspective is needed to see the way forward. Don't be fearful of taking charge and moving forward once the way is clear.

CHANGE OF PERSPECTIVE	LEADERSHIP, TAKING CHARGE
EXPLORE OTHER OPTIONS	PROVIDING OTHERS WITH DIRECTION
EXPAND HORIZONS	BEING AN EXAMPLE
HAVE FORESIGHT	REPRESENTATIVE
ANTICIPATING OBSTACLES	BEING IN A RESPONSIBLE POSITION
KNOW WHAT TO EXPECT	SEEK OUT THE UNKNOWN

Three of Wands - meaning & associations

SWORDS - Feelings such as sorrow and depression are deeply rooted in our state of mind. Again, it is for us to either allow these challenges to overcome and rule us, or we can build and grow from these. Having acquired a good balanced mindset allows us room to build a stable mental foundation to deal with Life's more difficult challenges. The Three of Swords is the epitome of sorrow and heart break, some of Life's harder lessons to deal with, but lessons we all need to experience and grow from.

BETRAYAL	SEPARATED
SORROW & DISAPPOINTMENT	PAINFUL TRUTH
BROKEN HEART	LETTING SOMEONE DOWN
DEAL WITH PAST HURTS	BEING LET DOWN
EMOTIONAL PAIN	MISPLACED TRUST
FEELING ALONE	HURT FEELINGS

Three of Swords - meaning & associations

Fours

So, we have found our balance, we've done some restructuring and we can now begin to build a solid foundation for ourselves. Fours are our chance to build something solid for us to stand on while we tackle the remainder of our Sub Journey. We cannot venture forward without a stable foundation. If we did everything would come crashing down and we would need to start again.

PENTACLES - Building a solid foundation for yourself to ensure your physical needs are being met is crucial. It is here that we decide what type of foundation we want. Is the foundation solely for the self and to serve the needs of the individual, or is the foundation to build a solid structure for others to utilise as well?0 A great side lesson in life is that we cannot control everyone and everything. We need to learn to let go and allow the flow of life to take control for us. We cannot allow our ego to dominate.

LETTING GO	LEARNING TO GIVE & TAKE
HANGING ON TO SOMEONE / SOMETHING	DEMANDING
DECLARING OWNERSHIP	WANTING COMPLIANCE
WANTING TO BE IN CHARGE	REFUSING CHANGE
SETTING RULES	OBSTRUCTING THE FLOW

Four of Pentacles - meaning & associations

CUPS - Having learnt about the emotions that come from both friendships and intimate relationships, we can withdraw and learn about our own core emotions. We must be wary of becoming too oblivious to what is going on around us though, as we may miss an opportunity to grow further in our emotional capacity. Life will always open doors or windows of opportunity, however if we are to focus within, we may miss these opportunities being handed to us. Self-reflection is a necessary aspect of our lives, but one must be wary of being too self-absorbed and missing out on Life's many golden opportunities.

MISSED OPPORTUNITIES	CONTEMPLATION
APATHY	WITHDRAWAL
FEELING DISCONNECTED	LACK OF MOTIVATION
BOREDOM	NO DESIRES
UNAWARE OF OTHERS	SELF-ABSORBED
INTROSPECTION	LOSS OF OUTER AWARENESS

Four of Cups - meaning & associations

WANDS - The time is now, we know what we want and how we can achieve our desires. We feel the energy flowing through us and we know that we're capable of big things. That feeling of true excitement - the type we experienced as children when receiving a present or the elation of getting something we desperately wanted. This feeling of excitement was often followed by a need for celebration as an indication of good things to come.

COMPLETION	BEING SURPRISED
WELL DESERVED REWARDS	RELISHING IN THE MOMENT
CAUSE FOR CELEBRATION	FEELING THRILLED OR JUBILANT
HAPPY EVENT	ACCOMPLISHMENTS
BREAKING FREE OF OPPRESSION	REACHING A MILESTONE
FEELINGS OF EXCITEMENT	HAVING POSITIVE EXPECTATIONS

Four of Wands - meaning & associations

SWORDS - After having dealt with difficulties of the mind, it is always a good decision to take some time out to ensure that we continue to build on a stable foundation. The mind is a delicate realm and needs to be treated gently until it has grown and has become stronger to deal with more challenging situations. Ensure you are building on a solid foundation that cannot easily be shaken. The suit of Swords is about challenges, which makes the Four of Swords seem strange. Why would a need for rest and stillness be a challenge? It can be a huge challenge for one who is over-wrought with trials and mental challenges, where the only answer is to simply stop, rest and recoup before starting afresh tomorrow.

NEED TO TAKE A BREAK	CHALLENGE LIES AHEAD
BODY NEEDS REST	QUIET PREPARATION
NEED TO CLEAR ONE'S MIND	TIME FOR CONTEMPLATION
GAIN A BETTER PERSPECTIVE	STEPPING OUT OF A SITUATION
TAKE THINGS EASY	GAINING STABILITY
GAINING STRENGTH	

Four of Swords - meaning & associations

Fives

Fives are there as a test. They test everything we have done up until this point. We have found balance, we moved things around so they work efficiently, and we have built a good solid foundation. Now it's time to see if they really are as stable as we thought. Fives make for a great challenge to test if we will cope with the rest of the lessons that will be brought to us in our Suit Journey. These are often those annoying and frustrating curveballs that Life throws at us. They are the proverbial spanners-in-the-works.

PENTACLES - From experiencing loss, we can fully understand gratitude and what it truly means to be wealthy - not in a monetary sense, but in a sense of fulfilment. This is the challenge of the Five of Pentacles. Most people have an innate fear of losing something, having poor health or having to go without. We must remember that as spiritual beings, we are whole and complete. We must accept it as our birthright to have all that we need, that we should set these fears aside and in times of loss or hardship, seek fulfilment from the spiritual.

HARDSHIPS	LACKING SECURITY
FEELING LEFT OUT IN THE COLD	FEELING EXCLUDED / ALONE
EXPERIENCING LOSS	REJECTION
ILLNESS OR POOR HEALTH	RECEIVING DISAPPROVAL
NEGLECTING YOUR BODY	LACK OF SUPPORT

Five of Pentacles - meaning & associations

CUPS - Grief is an emotion we will experience within our Lifetime, whether it is from the loss of a loved one, the end of a friendship, or even detaching from unnecessary emotions we may be carrying. Grief brings us a great lesson, one similar to that of the Five of Pentacles: only once we have learnt to go without, we can we really appreciate what or who we have. In dealing with loss, we often find it difficult to see beyond the sadness. One must remember that with loss of any kind, we must always maintain balance and see the situation from all sides, not just the negative and dark.

SUFFERING A LOSS	EXPERIENCING A SETBACK
CONSUMED BY WORRY	CRYING OVER SPILT MILK
FEELING SADNESS	GRIEF
PLAGUED BY DISAPPOINTMENTS	WRONG CHOICES
FEELING OVERWHELMED	ACKNOWLEDGING MISTAKES
HAVING REGRETS	

Five of Cups - meaning & associations

WANDS - The challenge of the Five of Wands is knowing where we should be putting our passion (energy), which battles are worth the fight and which ones are petty enough to be walked away from. Trivial annoyances and mundane day-to-day hassles often get the better of us. It sometimes feels as if everything is going wrong and the World is against you, but these are often a build-up of small or minor setbacks that can be easily overcome.

PETTY QUARRELS, ARGUMENTS	TRIVIAL PROBLEMS
MINOR OBSTACLES	TRYING TO OUT DO YOURSELF
COMPETIVENESS	RISING TO A CHALLENGE
LOOKING FOR A FIGHT	GOING AGAINST A RIVAL
BEING CHALLENGED	DISAGREEMENTS
MINOR SETBACKS	

Five of Wands - meaning & associations

SWORDS - The challenge of the Five of Swords is to teach us about strategy and common logic. We cannot go into battle holding all our weapons, we won't have the agility to defend ourselves as we would be too busy holding onto everything. Likewise, do not over-stress the mind with unnecessary clutter, be practical and strategic in your thinking and only hold onto what is essential in the mind. Through-out Life we all need to gauge when self-interest is required and when it is not. This is the challenge of the Five of Swords. If one is being too self-absorbed, it is time to expand their thinking beyond themselves. However, if the opposite is true, then one needs to start putting themselves first.

LOOKING OUT FOR YOURSELF	POWER STRUGGLES
THINKING OF ONE'S OWN INTERESTS	SACRIFICING INTEGRITY
LOSS OF MORAL COMPASS	CONFLICT
LOSING SIGHT OF WHATS RIGHT	STUCK IN A RUT
DISHONOURABLE	VICIOUS CYCLE
HOSTILE ENVIRONMENT	DISHONOUR

Five of Swords - meaning & associations

Sixes

The after-effects of the chaos caused by the Fives. Sixes represent a time when Life seems to move into a moment of calm. After weathering the storms of the Fives, we are strong enough to progress forward again, having gained valuable knowledge and understanding of the relevant core aspects that we should be dealing with at the time. We have found that our balance wasn't thrown out all that much and our foundation is still standing - we are still in one piece, and we can carry on.

PENTACLES - From having understood loss and the lessons that come with this experience, we can move on to understanding the true balance between giving and receiving. We also learn that we will always, in fact have enough regardless of our situation. The biggest lesson we can learn from experiencing hardships and loss is that we can learn to understand what it really means to have to go without. In learning this valuable lesson, we can look at life in retrospect and answer important questions.

GIVING / RECEIVING	HAVING / NOT HAVING POWER
TAKEN CARE OF / TAKING CARE OF	GIVING / RECEIVING INFORMATION
HAVING / NOT HAVING	GIVING / RECEIVING GENEROSITY
TEACHING / LEARNING	HAVING / NOT HAVING RESOURCES
GIVING ADVICE / RECEIVING ADVICE	

Six of Pentacles - meaning & associations

CUPS - The love and compassion of a child is immense; they are untainted by the negative aspects of the world, and they feel with such an innocence. We can also relearn how to love in this manner, particularly after having experienced grief and sadness. Allowing an unhappy experience to make us more loving and compassionate is a massive lesson. For as much as we have loss, anger, violence and many other 'negative' aspects to this life, we must never forget the innocence, purity and blessings we have on the flip side. The soft innocence of childhood is a great reminder of this, it gives us the warm feeling of happy nostalgia.

INNOCENCE	EXPERIENCING GOOD WILL
BLISSFULLY UNAWARE	BEING CHARITABLE
CHILDHOOD MEMORIES	BEING PLAYFUL
REUNIONS	ENJOYING THE SMALL THINGS
REMEMBERING OLD TIMES	WORKING WITH CHILDREN
NOSTALGIA	

Six of Cups - meaning & associations

WANDS - A true victory acknowledging and understanding the challenge of the Five. We are stepping in the right direction, and our passion is driving us forward. After tackling our minor obstacles and challenges, we will emerge victorious. All your hard work and efforts will start paying off and that competitive streak you have will count in your favor.

ACHIEVING SUCCESS	PUSHING THROUGH OBSTACLES
TRIUMPH	BEING ACKNOWLEDGED
RECEIVING GOOD NEWS	RECEIVING PRAISE OR RECOGNITION
RECEIVING REWARDS	HEALTHY SELF-ESTEEM
OVERCOMING CHALLENGES	HOLD YOUR HEAD HIGH
VINDICATION	SELF IMPORTANCE, ARROGANCE

Six of Wands - meaning & associations

SWORDS - Having cleared our minds of the unessential, we can begin to move forward once again, taking with us what is important. We are gaining good control over our mind and mastering our mental abilities. Things may seem to be stuck in limbo where one moves neither forwards nor backwards. However, this slow-paced journey does have an end in sight and one can count on reaching calm waters soon enough. One needs to pull themselves through and fight through the stagnation.

OVERCOME OBSTACLES	FEELING RESTLESS
BALANCE NEEDED	STAGNATION
HARMONY TO BE RESTORED	LEARNING TO COPE
MOVING TO A TIME OF PEACE	CHANGE OF SCENERY
CHANGE IN LOCATION	SENSE OF DEPRESSION
KEEPING HEAD ABOVE WATER	

Six of Swords - meaning & associations

Sevens

The strength to carry on. As we venture closer to the end of our Sub Journey, we can often find ourselves feeling bored or distracted with the process. Sevens are where we need to step back and review our situation.

PENTACLES - The time to assess your physical situation, to reflect on what you have experienced and learnt up till that point. From here you can choose to continue with the current path, or to venture off in a different direction. Reaping the fruits of our labor is highly rewarding and when reaching the end of a goal, those feelings of success are there to be enjoyed and reflected upon. It also indicates that it could be time for a change in direction, or time for a new project to commence.

ASSESSING A SITUATION	CHANGE IN DIRECTION
REFLECTING ON PROGRESS	CHECKING RESULTS
SEEING RESULTS	STANDING AT A CROSSROADS
REACHING A MILESTONE	EVALUATE BEFORE MAKING DECISION
ACHIEVING A GOAL	CONSIDER ALTERNATIVES

Seven of Pentacles - meaning & associations

CUPS - We are moving forward with Cups filled with various emotions and we are now able to step back and choose which emotions are serving us and which ones are worth letting go. It's time to assess our emotional state and decide who we are going to become from an emotional standpoint.

The Seven of Cups can be an indication that it's time to let it all go and stop being so controlling or it can indicate that it's time to start making some decisions and take charge of the situation.

STRONG COMPETITION	LACKING IN COMMITMENT
HAVING OPEN OPTIONS	NOT FOCUSSED
EVERYTHING UP IN THE AIR	TIME TO LET GO
DECISION TO BE MADE	LESS CONTROL IS NEEDED
ARRAY OF OPPORTUNITIES	PROCRASTINATING
IMAGINATION RUN WILD	BEING ABLE TO PICK & CHOOSE

Seven of Cups - meaning & associations

WANDS - Having the upper hand puts us in a great position to assess what is happening and consider our options for moving forward. It's time to take a stand, but ask yourself first, if this battle is worth fighting. If it is worth the fight, then you must believe in yourself and stand your ground. You will need strength and integrity in to order to progress from here.

STRONG COMPETITION	RESISTING AUTHORITY
DETERMINATION TO SUCCEED	STRENGTH OF CHARACTER
HAVE COURAGE	KNOWING YOU ARE RIGHT
SELF-ASSERTION	BEING SURE OF YOURSELF
BEING ON THE OFFENSIVE	DEFENDING YOUR POSITION
KNOWING HOW TO SAY NO	

Seven of Wands - meaning & associations

SWORDS - We are given an opportunity to test our new-found mental abilities of strategy and practicality. To move forward towards the end goal, we need to be smart about how we are going to get there. It's time to step back and see what the best strategy is for moving forward. The Seven of Swords is closely linked to the Five of Swords in that it also involves self-interest and separation from others. It's a clear indication that one is craving alone time to either avoid Life's challenges or to plan, strategies and work out how they wish to progress forward.

AVOIDING RESPONSIBILITIES	BEING ALOOF
A NEED TO BE ALONE	ALLOWING OTHERS TO TAKE THE FALL
AVOIDING OBLIGATIONS	AVOIDING A SHAMEFUL SITUATION
WANTING INDEPENDENCE	KEEPING OTHERS AT ARM'S LENGTH
TAKING THE EASY WAY OUT	HIDING FROM THE TRUTH

Seven of Swords - meaning & association

Eights

Once we have stepped back and assessed the situation, we can now wisely choose where we would like to go. Do we continue with the current path, having learnt what we do and don't need, are we are now prepared to let go of what is no longer necessary and hold tight to what is? Eights are our chance to use our knowledge and wisdom and decide if this is what we want and need, or if we are comfortable to abandon the current path to start on another that we know is right for us.

PENTACLES - It's time to choose what we want and where we want to go. Do we continue to work mindfully and with purpose on our current path, or do we see other options that may be available? Perseverance with current realistic goals will move you closer to achieving what you need and what you want. It is time to focus on the task at hand, give attention to detail and complete those projects. Tie-up loose-ends, ensure you put in 110% effort, and you'll hold the key to success.

HARD WORK BEING PAID OFF	BEING METHODICAL
GAINING NEW SKILLS	INCREASING KNOWLEDGE
BEING DILIGENT	ATTENTION TO DETAIL
PRODUCING RESULTS	SEEING THE FINER POINTS
BEING DEDICATED TO A TASK	TYING UP LOOSE-ENDS

Eight of Pentacles - meaning & associations

CUPS - Having assessed our emotional aspect, we now choose to walk away from what we no longer need. This can be actual emotional states we have decided we no longer need, or it could be relationships and friendships that no longer serve us. Knowing what is worth keeping and what is worth walking away from grows our emotional intelligence drastically. Nothing in life is permanent and we always reach points when it's time to move on. However, one must be wary of things unfinished or incomplete. When moving forward one needs to complete their current journey, or else they will travel forward holding onto unnecessary baggage.

LOSS OF INTEREST	LACK OF ENERGY OR HOPE
CLOSURE IS NEEDED	SEEKING ANSWERS
REALISING THE END OF A CYCLE	ESTABLISHING THE FACTS
FEELING EXHAUSTED	MOVING ON
WEARY OF A SITUATION	STARTING SOMETHING NEW
BEING DRAINED BY DEMANDS	CONCENTRATING ON THE IMPORTANT

Eight of Cups - meaning & associations

WANDS - Having considered the way forward and planned how we are going to get there, we are ready to launch onto that path with a swift determination and a lot of passion. Things begin to move forward at a rapid rate, and we seem to be charging towards our goal. The time is now, and swift action is required. Now is not the time for hesitation, one must be fully aware of all that is happening around them to avoid being swept away by the coming change.

MAKE YOUR MOVE, TAKE ACTION	OBTAINING MUCH NEED INFORMATION
PUT PLANS INTO ACTION	HAVING EVERYTHING YOU REQUIRE
SUDDEN CHANGE	RECEIVING IMPORTANT NEWS
DON'T DELAY	LEARNING THE TRUTH
FAST ACTION IS REQUIRED	SPONTANEITY
REACHING A CONCLUSION	

Eight of Wands - meaning & associations

SWORDS – After having established a way forward, we find we are faced once again with the challenge of fear. We know how to move forward, but it just feels too big and scary. We need to decide if we are going to allow these fears to hold us back or if we are going to overpower those fears and move forward regardless. In dealing with some of Life's challenges we can often feel lost, trapped and very alone. Held in place by our own doubts and fears, these situations can make it seem as though we have no choices, and we end up feeling restricted. But one must remember that Life is all about choices and we can choose to continue feeling trapped or we can choose to remove those bonds and continue moving forward.

FEELING TRAPPED OR RESTRICTED	CONFUSION
BEING BLIND TO THE WAY FORWARD	FEELING OVERWHELMED
BLINDED BY FEAR	LACKING DIRECTION
POWERLESS	FEELING LITTLE CHOICE
VICTIMISED	NEED FOR CLARITY
REFUSING RESPONSIBILITY	LACKING GUIDANCE

Eight of Swords - meaning & associations

Nines

Nines are the consequences of our decisions made in the Eights. We have either chosen to continue the current path or to walk away from it. It is now time to handle the consequences of our decisions. These may be highly positive if the path we are choosing is optimistic and easy enough to handle, or they may instil a certain level io fear if the path we have chosen is big and scary. But will be worth it in the end.

PENTACLES - There is a theory that while we are growing up, we are dependent on our parents/caregivers to give us what we need. As we begin to approach adulthood, we start to claim our independence. The decisions we made at the Eight of Pentacles will determine how we achieve this and outline what out perception of independence is. The Nine of Pentacles is when you become your definition of self-reliant. Mastering our independence is one of the more gratifying lessons we learn along our life path. It is where we learn about ourselves and what we will and will not accept. It is where we truly become who we are and who choose to be.

FINANCIAL INDEPENDENCE	HAVING SELF CONTROL
ENJOY ONE'S OWN COMPANY	COMFORTABLE LIFESTYLE
COMFORTABLE WITH YOURSELF	DIPLOMACY & TACT
MASTERING SELF DISCIPLINE	ENJOYING THE FINER THINGS
SELF-RELIANCE	ENJOYING HIGH-MINDED ACTIVITIES

Nine of Pentacles - meaning & associations

CUPS - We are now already becoming our own person: we have kept emotions that work for us, and we are well equipped to walk forward in life, being able to truly experience everything from an emotional perspective; without the threat of being overly emotional or expressing unnecessary emotions. We are taking charge of our emotions and allowing this to make us stronger. One will always feel a sense of self-satisfaction when they realize that they have all they require to achieve their goals and ambitions. It's time to put plans into action and see the fruits of your labor.

EMOTIONAL ACHIEVEMENT	DESIRE TO SHARE
HAVING ALL THAT IS REQUIRED	ACHIEVING SUCCESS
WISHES FULFILLED	SELF-SATISFACTION
ACHIEVING GOALS	FEELING AT PEACE
ATTAINING DESIRES	EXPERIENCING LUXURY
BEING CONTENT	

Nine of Cups - meaning & associations

WANDS - Sometimes we bump our heads along the way. This can often be the case when we are charging towards a goal, and we are almost oblivious to anything else. The Nine is a reminder that these little bumps are sometimes needed so that we can maintain awareness moving forward - to see the whole picture and not just the result. In times of despair, ill health or bad experiences, we find ourselves being wary and guarded. We keep our defences up, trying to avoid any further damage. In these times, one must keep their strength and not guardedness or defensiveness.

EXPECTING THE WORST	FIGHTING THE GOOD FIGHT
BEING DEFENSIVE	BEING GUARDED
TAKING PRECAUTIONS	PERSEVERANCE IS NEEDED
HAVE STRENGTH OF WILL	KEEP YOUR RESOLVE
STAMINA IS REQUIRED	GET BACK UP WHEN KNOCKED DOWN
DRAW ON RESERVES	

Nine of Wands - meaning & associations

SWORDS - It is time to deal with the consequences of our decisions of the Eight. We cannot however allow these decisions to haunt us, and we cannot question ourselves after the fact. We have made our decisions, and we need to keep moving forward. We cannot obsess over those choices and allow them to fill our heads with doubts. In the quietest hours of night, we wake, our minds whirling, gripped by fears, worry or doubts. This is the Nine of Swords, our sleepless nights filled with thoughts of "Is this right?" or "Am I making the right choices?"

We feel trapped and burdened by stresses; how does one get out of this nightmare?

DOUBTS	DEPRESSION
FEARS AND WORRIES	FEAR OF FAILURE
HARPING ON AN ISSUE	FEELING DESPAIR
FEELINGS OF GUILT	SLEEPLESS NIGHTS
REGRETS	TOO HARD ON YOURSELF
ANXIETY	FEELINGS OF REMORSE

Nine of Swords - meaning & associations

Tens

The end of the cycle. We have reached the final stage in our Sub Journey. It is now time to take the lessons learnt and apply them practically to our main Soul Journey so that we may become wiser and more enlightened.

PENTACLES - So we have achieved our version of independence, and we have come full circle. The Ten of Pentacles is about inter-dependence, where we learn to live in balanced co-existence with others. Our Sub Journey through the Suit of Pentacles has taught us the beautiful lessons of the Earth, that we need to have a balanced, stable foundation on which to build, not only for yourself, but for those who matter so that we can all achieve a stable and balanced co-existence. We will, all at stages in our lives, reach points of stability and security, where we have finally built that solid foundation and now it is time to revel in the rewards.

FINANCIAL SECURITY	STAYING WITH THE TRIED-&-TESTED ROUTES
ACHIEVING STABILITY	HAVING ESTABLISHED GUIDELINES
ENJOYING SUCCESS	FREEDOM FROM MONETARY PROBLEMS
ABUNDANCE	HAVING A PERMANENT SOLUTION
SOLID FOUNDATION	HAVING A SUCCESSFUL LONG TERM PLAN

Ten of Pentacles - meaning & associations

CUPS - Our Sub Journey through our emotional side is complete, we find we have everything we need and feel full and content. Life is true bliss, and we have established our white picket fence with those that matter. Everyone's white picket fence is different, but it is always based on having happiness, contentment and a loving family to experience it with. The time for peace and abundant blessings has arrived for you and your family.

SENSE OF WELL-BEING	CONTENTMENT
LASTING HAPPINESS	HARMONY BEING RESTORED
COUNT YOUR BLESSINGS	FAMILY SUPPORT
ESTABLISH PEACE IN THE HOME	FORGIVENESS WITHIN THE FAMILY
BONDING WITH FAMILY MEMBERS	REDUCING STRESS & TENSION
FEELING SERENE	

Ten of Cups - meaning & associations

WANDS - That moment when we see our goal is in sight and completion has arrived. We have reached our destination for our

Sub Journey, we have utilised our energy and passion wisely and we can begin to reap the rewards. That uphill battle will be worth it, keep putting in the work and effort and you will be rewarded. Ensure however, that you are not overworking yourself unnecessarily and focus on maintaining an adequate balance.

LEARN TO SAY NO	BEING HELD ACCOUNTABLE
TRYING TO TAKE ON TO MUCH	SADDLED WITH ALL THE WORK
BEING OVER BURDENED	CLEANING UP A MESSY SITUATION
UPHILL BATTLES	PUSHING THROUGH
TAKING RESPONSIBILITY	PERSEVERANCE
DOING WHAT IS REQUIRED	

Ten of Wands - meaning & associations

SWORDS - Learning that there is no such thing as a bad decision will allow us to pick ourselves back up again when we find we have hit rock bottom. We have dealt with the consequences of the Eight and we need to dust ourselves off and carry on. Having achieved this, we have mastered the Sub Journey of the mind. Things cannot get any worse than the Ten of Swords, it's the proverbial rock bottom. However, one must be wary of 'victim-based' attitudes or martyrdom. When hitting rock bottom, it is a sure sign that things can only go up from here. If one has a 'poor-me' mentality or is being a martyr about the situation then they may as well just continue to lie there and be uncomfortable.

MISERY	PUTTING OTHERS FIRST
HITTING ROCK BOTTOM	LACKING SELF CARE
FEELING POWERLESS	DARKEST BEFORE DAWN
PLAYING THE VICTIM	SELF-PITY
UNNECESSARY SACRIFICES	WAITING FOR BETTER DAYS
ACTING LIKE A DOORMAT	PUSH OVER

Ten of Swords - meaning & associations

Chapter 11

The Court Cards

The Court Cards can be some of the most insightful yet challenging cards to work with. They represent archetypal personalities, energies and dynamic aspects of situations. Some may feel familiar, while others may seem distant or even triggering. Engaging with each suit and each Court Card individually is a valuable exercise in self-reflection and understanding. Working with them for self-betterment - integrating their balanced aspects - can be deeply rewarding, offering an expanded perspective on personal growth and interactions with others. If the Courts feel overwhelming, know that this is common. Many of my students have struggled with them in the past, and I am always happy to help if you feel stuck.

In readings, Court Cards serve multiple roles. They can represent people, aspects of personality, energetic influences or even events and situations. Their meaning depends on the context - sometimes they reflect external figures, while other times they highlight qualities within the self that need to be developed or understood. Recognizing this fluidity is key to working with them effectively.

The elemental associations of the Minor Arcana carry through into the Court Cards, but each rank also has an additional elemental correspondence that influences its energy. Pages, Knights, Queens and Kings each embody a different level of maturity, approach and interaction with the world. While there are general connections to genders and age groups, these are symbolic rather than fixed.

Astrology can also provide insight into the Court Cards. While there are no set numerological or astrological associations, the twelve zodiac signs can be referenced when exploring personality traits. Pages are typically not associated with astrology, whereas Knights, Queens and Kings have traditional correspondences. However, these are not rigid assignments - if a particular Court Card resonates differently for you, trust your intuition. For example, if the Queen of Wands feels more like Leo than Aries to you, then work with that understanding.

Interpreting Court Cards requires flexibility. They can signify specific people, broader personality traits, shifting energies or the dynamics at play in a situation. Context is everything. Are they representing an external influence, a part of yourself or the way a situation is unfolding? Asking these questions in a reading helps unlock their deeper meaning. Understanding the Courts is a skill that develops over time, and with practice, they become some of the most valuable and insightful cards in the deck.

Pentacles

The personality of Pentacles is deeply grounded. They are practical, value stability and are often seen as reserved or introverted. Beneath this, they are deeply committed, sometimes to the point of stubbornness. Pentacles are loyal, focused and hard-working, with a strong connection to nature and a passion for the outdoors.

EARTH ELEMENT | GROUNDED
CAPRICORN | VIRGO | TAURUS

STABLE	COMMITTED
LOYAL	SLOW TO ANGER
ENTREPRENEUR	PRACTICAL
MATERIALISTIC	FAMILY CENTRED

Pentacles element & suit breakdown

Page of Pentacles – A student of life, eager to learn and grow. The Page of Pentacles represents curiosity, discipline and a practical approach to new opportunities. They are methodical and patient, willing to take the necessary steps toward success.

PERSONALITY	EVENTS & SITUATIONS	ADDITONAL ASSOCIATIONS	
SCHOLARLY	NEW IDEAS	SUIT ELEMENT	- EARTH
CAUTIOUS	NEW BUSINESS OPPORTUNITIES	RANK ELEMENT	- EARTH
LOYAL	TIME FOR PRACTICALITY	ENERGY	- FEMININE
RESERVED	TIME OF PROSPERITY	AGE GROUP	- CHILDREN
INTROVERTED	BE REALISTIC	ASTROLOGY	- NONE
STUBBORN	STAND BY YOUR COMMITMENTS		
COMMITTED	GAIN CREDIBILITY		
SECURE	ENRICHMENT		

Page of Pentacles meanings

Knight of Pentacles – The most steady and reliable of the Knights, this figure represents persistence, responsibility and diligence. While not one for impulsiveness, the Knight of Pentacles ensures that work is done properly, and commitments are honored.

PERSONALITY	EVENTS & SITUATIONS	ADDITONAL ASSOCIATIONS	
HARD WORKING	STEADY PROGRESS	SUIT ELEMENT	- EARTH
TRUSTWORTHY	TAKING ON RESPONSIBILITIES	RANK ELEMENT	- FIRE
PATIENT	THE TASK AT HAND	ENERGY	- MASCULINE
LOVER OF NATURE	WRAP UP LOOSE ENDS	AGE GROUP	- ADOLESCENT
NARROW MINDED	KNOW WHEN TO QUIT	ASTROLOGY	- CAPRICORN
REALISTIC	FOCUS ON RIGHT GOALS		
THOROUGH	EXAMINE ALL ANGLES		
UNADVENTUROUS	LISTEN TO REASON		

Knight of Pentacles meanings

Queen of Pentacles – A nurturing provider, the Queen of Pentacles embodies abundance, practicality and generosity. She creates stability, tending to both material and emotional needs with care and wisdom.

PERSONALITY	EVENTS & SITUATIONS	ADDITONAL ASSOCIATIONS	
NURTURING	BE SENSIBLE	SUIT ELEMENT	- EARTH
BUSINESS MINDED	USE RESOURCES YOU HAVE	RANK ELEMENT	- WATER
UTILISES TALENTS	TIME FOR ACCOMPLISHMENT	ENERGY	- FEMININE
DOWN TO EARTH	HAVE NO PRETENCES	AGE GROUP	- ADULT
TRUSTWORTHY	HAVE REALISTIC EXPECTATIONS	ASTROLOGY	- VIRGO
RESOURCEFUL	BE SELF NURTURING		
BIG HEART	BE CARING		
CARING & GENTLE	BE SIMPLE & SENSIBLE		

Queen of Pentacles meanings

King of Pentacles – The master of material success, the King of Pentacles represents security, leadership and long-term planning. He builds and maintains wealth, focusing on sustainability and legacy.

PERSONALITY	EVENTS & SITUATIONS	ADDITONAL ASSOCIATIONS	
LIKES SECURITY	BUILDING SECURITY	SUIT ELEMENT	- EARTH
GOOD BUSINESS SENSE	INCREASES IN MATERIAL	RANK ELEMENT	- AIR
CAUTIOUS	CLIMBING THE LADDER	ENERGY	- MASCULINE
GREAT MONEY SKILLS	ATTAINING SUCCESS	AGE GROUP	- ADULT
RELIABLE	BE CAUTIOUS BUT ACT	ASTROLOGY	- TAURUS
ENTERPRISING	FIND SUPPORT		
SUPPORTIVE	STAY COMMITTED		
COMMITTED	USE OF SKILLS		

King of Pentacles meanings

Cups

The personality of Cups is soft, loving and deeply connected to emotions. They are guided by their feelings and show great care for the well-being of others. As intuitive beings, they navigate life through their hearts, often seen as romantics, philosophers and dreamers.

WATER ELEMENT | INTUITIVE
PISCES | CANCER | SCORPIO

GENEROUS	EMOTIONAL
LOVING	DEEP
CONNECTED	COMPASSIONATE
NURTURING	EMPATHIC

Cups element & suit breakdown

Page of Cups – A messenger of creativity and emotional openness, the Page of Cups represents innocence, imagination and the willingness to embrace feelings. They see the world with wonder and approach life with curiosity.

PERSONALITY	EVENTS & SITUATIONS	ADDITONAL ASSOCIATIONS	
SENSITIVE	LET YOUR FEELINGS SHOW	SUIT ELEMENT	- WATER
EMOTIONAL	LET YOUR HEART GUIDE YOU	RANK ELEMENT	- EARTH
INTUITIVE	TRUST YOUR INSTINCTS	ENERGY	- FEMININE
LOVING	LOOK WITHIN FOR GUIDANCE	AGE GROUP	- CHILDREN
CARING	RESPOND IN A CARING MANNER	ASTROLOGY	- NONE
GENTLE	DON'T BE QUICK TO JUDGE		
THOUGHTFUL	TIME FOR APOLOGIES		
HEALING	STRENGTHEN A BOND		

Page of Cups meanings

Knight of Cups – The idealist and romantic, the Knight of Cups follows his heart fearlessly. He is a dreamer, a poet and a seeker of beauty, though at times, his emotions can lead him to act impulsively.

PERSONALITY	EVENTS & SITUATIONS	ADDITONAL ASSOCIATIONS	
ROMANTIC	NEW EMOTIONAL MATTERS	SUIT ELEMENT	- WATER
IMAGINATIVE	EMPHASISE FEELINGS	RANK ELEMENT	- FIRE
PHILOSOPHICAL	PLEASANT ENVIRONMENT	ENERGY	- MASCULINE
VISIONARY	LOOK BEYOND THE OBVIOUS	AGE GROUP	- ADOLESCENT
DREAMER	TIME FOR TACT & DIPLOMACY	ASTROLOGY	- PISCES
APPRECIATIES BEAUTY	BE UNDERSTANDING		
EMPATHETIC	TIME FOR SELF-IMPROVEMENT		
INTROSPECTIVE	TIME FOR INTROSPECTION		

Knight of Cups meanings

Queen of Cups – The embodiment of intuition and compassion, the Queen of Cups offers deep emotional understanding. She is nurturing, wise and connected to the unseen, allowing emotions to flow naturally.

PERSONALITY	EVENTS & SITUATIONS	ADDITONAL ASSOCIATIONS	
HEALER	AVOID HARSH SITUATIONS	SUIT ELEMENT	- WATER
MOTHERLY	STRENGTHENED RELATIONSHIPS	RANK ELEMENT	- WATER
SOOTHING	TRUST YOUR INTUITION	ENERGY	- FEMININE
INTUITIVE	SHOW COMPASSION	AGE GROUP	- ADULT
SPIRITUAL	BE UNCONDITIONAL	ASTROLOGY	- CANCER
NATURAL MEDIUM	SEEK THE SPIRITUAL		
TUNED-IN	LOOK FOR DEEPER MEANING		
UNCONDITIONAL	BE EMPATHETIC		

Queen of Cups meanings

King of Cups – A figure of emotional maturity and wisdom, the King of Cups balances heart and mind. He leads with compassion and stability, offering guidance without being overwhelmed by emotions.

PERSONALITY	EVENTS & SITUATIONS	ADDITONAL ASSOCIATIONS	
CONSIDERATE	SEEK BETTER ADVICE	SUIT ELEMENT	- WATER
INTUITIVE	FAIRNESS IS NEEDED	RANK ELEMENT	- AIR
FATHERLY	MAINTAIN COMPOSURE	ENERGY	- MASCULINE
WISE	BE OPEN MINDED	AGE GROUP	- ADULT
TOLERANT	PATIENCE IS REQUIRED	ASTROLOGY	- SCORPIO
CALM	TAKE ACTION TO HELP OTHERS		
CARING	SEE THE HEART OF THE MATTER		
GENEROUS	REMAIN DIPLOMATIC		

King of Cups meanings

Wands

The personality of Wands is pure passion and fire. They are lively, adventurous and outgoing. Confident and sociable, Wands are natural leaders who make life happen rather than wait for it to unfold. They thrive in action, creativity and exploration.

FIRE ELEMENT | PASSIONATE
SAGITTARIUS | LEO | ARIES

ADVENTUROUS   CREATIVE
CONFIDENT   ARROGANT
FIERY   EASY TO ANGER
COURAGEOUS   OUTGOING

Wands element & suit breakdown

Page of Wands – The spark of inspiration, the Page of Wands represents enthusiasm, excitement and the willingness to take risks. They are full of energy and eager for adventure.

PERSONALITY	EVENTS & SITUATIONS	ADDITONAL ASSOCIATIONS	
INDEPENDENT	GOOD NEWS	SUIT ELEMENT	- FIRE
FIERY	OPEN COMMUNICATION	RANK ELEMENT	- EARTH
INDEPENDENT	CHANGE OF DIRECTION	ENERGY	- FEMININE
ENTHUSIASTIC	TACKLE THE CHALLENGE	AGE GROUP	- CHILDREN
CREATIVE	TAKE A DIFFERENT APPROACH	ASTROLOGY	- NONE
CONFIDENT	WORTH THE RISK		
ADVENTUROUS	BE ASSERTIVE		
OPTIMISTIC	TIME FOR LEADERSHIP		

Page of Wands meanings

Knight of Wands – A bold and impulsive figure, the Knight of Wands is driven by ambition and a desire for experience. He thrives on momentum but can sometimes act without thinking.

PERSONALITY	EVENTS & SITUATIONS	ADDITONAL ASSOCIATIONS	
CHARMING	CHANGE OF RESIDENCE	SUIT ELEMENT	- FIRE
YOUNG AT HEART	START OF A JOURNEY	RANK ELEMENT	- FIRE
PLAYFUL	BE DARING	ENERGY	- MASCULINE
FUN LOVING	DON'T DOUBT ABILITIES	AGE GROUP	- ADOLESCENT
GO GETTER	DON'T PRESUME	ASTROLOGY	- SAGITTARIUS
GENEROUS	AVOID BAD TEMPEREDNESS		
PASSIONATE	MAKE THINGS HAPPEN		
SELF-CONFIDENT	TIME FOR CHANGE		

Knight of Wands meanings

Queen of Wands – The Queen of Wands exudes confidence, independence and charisma. She is warm, inspiring and unafraid to take up space, leading with strength and enthusiasm.

PERSONALITY	EVENTS & SITUATIONS	ADDITONAL ASSOCIATIONS	
FRIENDLY	POWERFUL IMPRESSION	SUIT ELEMENT	- FIRE
EXCELLENT HOSTESS	ACHIEVEMENT	RANK ELEMENT	- WATER
SOCIABLE	DON'T HOLD ANYTHING BACK	ENERGY	- FEMININE
SUNNY DISPOSITION	HANDLE WITH SELF-ASSURANCE	AGE GROUP	- ADULT
WHOLEHEARTED	HAVE FAITH IN YOURSELF	ASTROLOGY	- LEO
ENERGETIC	BE DEDICATED TO THE TASK		
SELF-ASSURED	BE OPEN & SINCERE		
CHEERFUL	LOOK FOR INSPIRATION		

Queen of Wands meanings

King of Wands – A visionary and leader, the King of Wands represents authority, determination and influence. He sees the bigger picture and inspires others through action and presence.

PERSONALITY	EVENTS & SITUATIONS	ADDITONAL ASSOCIATIONS	
CHARISMATIC	WORK ON INNOVATION	SUIT ELEMENT	- FIRE
BOLD	TAKE THE LEAD	RANK ELEMENT	- AIR
INSPIRING	MAKE YOUR MOVE	ENERGY	- MASCULINE
GENTLEMAN	EARN RESPECT OF PEERS	AGE GROUP	- ADULT
BOSSY	SET AN EXAMPLE	ASTROLOGY	- ARIES
LEADER	COURAGE IS NEEDED		
SELF-ASSURED	TRY NOT TO DOMINATE		
FORCEFUL	NEW STRATEGIES		

King of Wands meanings

Swords

The personality of Swords is sharp, analytical and intellectually driven. They are deep thinkers, valuing logic, fairness and ethical reasoning. With a strong sense of justice, Swords seek truth and clarity, making them excellent strategists and problem solvers.

AIR ELEMENT | INTELLECTUAL
LIBRA | GEMINI | AQUARIUS

ANALYTICAL	MANIPULATIVE
ETHICAL	NARCISSITIC
COLD	INVENTIVE
INNOVATIVE	DEEP THINKERS

Swords element & suit breakdown

Page of Swords – The seeker of knowledge, the Page of Swords is curious, observant and quick-witted. They are always questioning, learning and analyzing the world around them.

PERSONALITY	EVENTS & SITUATIONS	ADDITONAL ASSOCIATIONS	
QUICK WIT	ANALYZE THE SITUATION	SUIT ELEMENT	- AIR
HIGH INTELLIGENCE	BE LOGICAL & REASONABLE	RANK ELEMENT	- EARTH
DIPLOMATIC	SPEAK DIRECTLY	ENERGY	- FEMININE
LOGICAL	THINK THINGS THROUGH	AGE GROUP	- CHILDREN
DOES THE RIGHT THING	THINK BEFORE ACTING	ASTROLOGY	- NONE
STRONG CHARACTER	FACE THE SITUATION HEAD ON		
REFUSES TO GIVE UP	BE PREPARED		
HEAD STRONG	OVERCOME OBSTACLES		

Page of Swords meanings

Knight of Swords – Fast-moving and highly determined, the Knight of Swords charges ahead with clear intent. He is bold and assertive, though sometimes impulsive in his pursuit of truth.

PERSONALITY	EVENTS & SITUATIONS	ADDITONAL ASSOCIATIONS	
QUICK MINDED	CHANGE OF EVENTS	SUIT ELEMENT	- AIR
LEADER	BE DIRECT & TO THE POINT	RANK ELEMENT	- FIRE
INNOVATIVE	HAVE FULL KNOWLEDGE	ENERGY	- MASCULINE
STRONG WILLED	CLEAR REASONING	AGE GROUP	- ADOLESCENT
SKILLFUL	SUDDEN CHANGE	ASTROLOGY	- LIBRA
IMPULSIVE	CLEAR UP CONFUSION		
DIRECT	BE ANALYTICAL		
KNOWLEDGEABLE	PRIORITISE		

Knight of Swords meanings

Queen of Swords – A figure of wisdom and independence, the Queen of Swords values honesty and discernment. She sees through deception and speaks with clarity, using intellect over emotion.

PERSONALITY	EVENTS & SITUATIONS	ADDITONAL ASSOCIATIONS	
PROFESSIONAL	SEIZE AN OPPORTUNITY	SUIT ELEMENT	- AIR
DEEP THINKER	QUICK DECISIONS	RANK ELEMENT	- WATER
STRONG WILLED	NEW MIND SET IS NEEDED	ENERGY	- FEMININE
HONEST	FACE THE TRUTH	AGE GROUP	- ADULT
WELL EXPERIENCED	BE DIRECT & OPEN	ASTROLOGY	- GEMINI
HIGH INTELLIGENCE	ACT WITHOUT PRETENCE		
ASTUTE	STICK TO THE RULES		
RIGHTEOUS	TAKE NO NONSENSE		

Queen of Swords meanings

King of Swords – The master of strategy and authority, the King of Swords represents strong leadership, discipline and fairness. He rules with intellect, making decisions based on logic and principle.

PERSONALITY	EVENTS & SITUATIONS	ADDITONAL ASSOCIATIONS	
ANALYTICAL	CHANGE IN PERSPECTIVE	SUIT ELEMENT	- AIR
CLEAR MINDED	BE INSPIRED BY THE CHALLENGES	RANK ELEMENT	- AIR
BUSINESS ACUMEN	BE ANALYTICAL	ENERGY	- MASCULINE
TO THE POINT	COMMUNICATE YOUR IDEAS	AGE GROUP	- ADULT
JUST & FAIR	IMPROVE SKILLS	ASTROLOGY	- AQUARIUS
HIGH INTELLIGENCE	MAKE INSIGHTFUL JUDGEMENT CALLS		
ETHICAL	ENCOURAGE HIGH STANDARDS		
RIGHTEOUS	MAINTAIN MORALS & ETHICS		

King of Swords meanings

Chapter 12
Card Associations

ALCHEMY ✶ ASTROLOGY ✶ ELEMENTS

AIR
THE MIND ASPECT
KNOWLEDGE
LEARNING

ANTIMONY
FREE SPIRITED
INSTINCTUAL
WILD NATURE

AQUARIUS
REVOLUTIONARY THINKING
RADICAL CHANGE
HUMANITARIAN

ARIES
FAST ACTION
DETERMINATION
FIERY SPIRIT

BRASS
INNER TRUTH
GENUINE
GOOD NATURED

BRIMSTONE
PURIFICATION
TRANSITIONING
BURNING THROUGH

CANCER
RELATIONSHIP TIES
EMOTIONAL ASPECT
SENSITIVE NATURE

CAPRICORN
TENACITY
DOMINANCE
PERSEVERANCE

EARTH
STRUCTURE
FOUNDATION
STABILITY

ELEMENTS
BALANCE
HARMONY
ORDER

FIRE
CREATION
DESTRUCTION
PASSION

GEMINI
DUALITY
FLEXIBILITY
INDECISION

GLASS
FRAGILITY
VULNERABILITY
DELICATE NATURE

IRON
DESTRUCTION
CONSTRUCTION
FORCE

JUPITER/TIN
ENTHUSIASM
GENEROSITY
SEEKING KNOWLEDGE

LEO
COURAGE
POWER
STRENGTH

LIBRA
BALANCE
JUSTICE
FAIRNESS

MARS/IRON
FORCEFUL
FOCUS
ASSERTIVE

MERCURY
VERSATILITY
PERCEPTIVENESS
COMMUNICATION

MOON
INTUITION
CYCLES
MYSTERIES

NEPTUNE
ENLIGHTENMENT
DISTORTION
FINDING FLOW

PISCES
TRUTH
DEPTH
IMAGINATION

PLATINUM
ENDURANCE
DETERMINATION
MANIFESTATIONS

PLUTO
MASTERY
EXPERIENCE
TRANSFORMATION

SAGITTARIUS
OPTIMISM
ADVENTUROUS / OPEN
PHILOSOPHICAL

SALT
BREAKING DOWN
STRIPING AWAY
CLEARING

SATURN/LEAD
STABILITY
DISCIPLINE
ACCOMPLISHMENT

SCORPIO
PURPOSE
TRANSITION
INTUITION

SILVER
VERSATILITY
PHILOSOPHY
EMOTIONAL ASPECT

SQUARED CIRCLE
PHILOSOPHERS STONE
ELEMENTAL BALANCE
MASTER

STEEL
STRENGTH
PERSISTENCE
AWARENESS

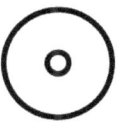

SULFUR
PURIFICATION
TRANSITIONING
BURNING THROUGH

SUN/GOLD
VITALITY
ENLIGHTENMENT
TRANSFORMATION

TAURUS
DURABILITY
STAMINA
STUBBORNNESS

URANUS
CHANGES
BEGINNINGS
SELF EXPRESSION

VENUS/COPPER
NURTURING
ABUNDANCE
FEMININITY

VIRGO
OBSERVATION
PRACTICALITY
OPINIONATED

WATER
EMOTIONS
INTUITION
NATURAL FLOW

COLORS

BLACK
FORCE
STRENGTH
HEAVINESS

PINK
KINDNESS
NURTURE
TENDERNESS

BLUE
FREEDOM
SENSITIVITY
IMAGINATION

PURPLE
SPIRITUALITY
HIGHER THINKING
ENLIGHTENMENT

BROWN
GROUNDED
STABILITY
PRACTICAL

RAINBOW
UNITY
HOPE
CONNECTION

GREEN
NATURE
GROWTH
HEALTH

RED
ACTION
PASSION
RADIANCE

GREY
MYSTERY
UNCERTAINTY
HIDDEN KNOWLEDGE

WHITE
PEACE
PURITY
TRANQUIL

ORANGE
WISDOM
TRANQUILITY
COMPASSION

YELLOW
WARMTH
CLARITY
POSITIVITY

FIGURES * OBJECTS

ANGEL
DIVINE MESSAGE
ASSISTANCE
PROTECTION

ANUBIS
LINK BETWEEN WORLDS
LIFE/DEATH CYCLE
TRANSFORMATION

ARCH
OPENINGS
NEW DIRECTION
OPPORTUNITIES

ARMOR
PROTECTION
STRENGTH
DEFENSE

BENCH
CONTEMPLATION
EXPLORE OPTIONS
REFLECTION

BLINDFOLD
BLIND TO FACTS
REFUSING TO SEE
AVOIDING TRUTH

BOAT
MOVEMENT
SLOW PROGRESS
CHANGE IN DIRECTION

BRICK WALL
HOLDING BACK
PROTECTION
STOPPING FLOW

BRIDGE
PROGRESS
HELP IS THERE
CONNECTION

BUDDHA
WISDOM
INNER PEACE
COMPASSION

CASTLE
ATTAINMENT
AMBITION
STRONGHOLD

CHAINS
BINDING
ADDICTIONS
FEELING TRAPPED

CHARIOT
DEDICATION
MASTERED CONTROL
SELF MASTERY

CHILDREN
HOPE
CURIOSITY
INNOCENCE

CITY/TOWN
GATHERING OF ENERGY
COLLECTIVE CONSCIOUS
COMMON GOALS

COMPASS
DIRECTION
TRUE NORTH
DISCOVERY

CROW
INTELLIGENCE
TRANSFORMATION
INTEGRITY

CUP
EMOTIONS
FULFILLMENT
EMPTINESS

DANCER
CELEBRATION
FREEDOM
EXPRESSION

DICE
LUCK
CHANCE
RISKS

DRAGON
POWER
STRENGTH
FORCE

DOOR
OPPORTUNITY
STEPPING OUT
CLOSED OFF

EGG
BIRTH
PURITY
BEGINNING

EYE
INNER SIGHT
GATEWAY
HONESTY

FAIRY/PIXIE
MAGIC
PLAYFULNESS
INNOCENCE

FAMILY
LOVE
SUPPORT
HERITAGE

FAN
ROYALTY
OPEN/CLOSED
SOPHISTICATION

FLAG
ANNOUNCES CHANGE
BIG TRANSFORMATION
LARGE SCALE MOVEMENT

GAIA/MOTHER EARTH
NURTURING
ABUNDANCE
LIFE FORCE

GUARD/WARRIOR
PROTECTION
INTEGRITY
HONOR

GODS
ACTION
POWER
FORCE

GODDESS
BEAUTY
STRENGTH
COMPASSION

HAMMER
HAMMERING A POINT
WORKING IN PROGRESS
BUILDING/DESTROYING

HAND
ASSISTANCE
HELPING HAND
RECEIVING/GIVING

HOE/PLOUGH
RESOURCEFULNESS
HAVING THE TOOLS
REAPING WHAT YOU SOW

HORN/TRUMPET
TRIUMPH
VICTORY
ANNOUNCEMENT

HOUSE
GUARDED/SAFE
FAMILY MATTERS
HEART MATTERS

ISIS
MOTHER
LIFE/DEATH
HEALING

JESTER
FOOLISH
LIGHT HEARTED
GOOD NATURED

JEWELS/GEMS
WEALTH
POSSESSIONS
SOPHISTICATION

KEY
UNLOCKING SECRETS
RECEIVING KNOWLEDGE
REVEALING THE HIDDEN

KING
AUTHORITY
FAIRNESS
DISCIPLINE

LADDER
DIVINE CONNECTION
ASCENSION
PROGRESS

LANTERN/LIGHT
GUIDANCE
ILLUMINATION
ENLIGHTENMENT

MASK
MYSTERY
SECRETIVE
DISGUISES

PILLARS
BALANCE
EQUALITY
FAIRNESS

PITCHER
WHAT WE HOLD ONTO
WHAT WE PUT FORTH
WHAT FILLS US UP

POPE/PRIEST
BELIEFS
TRADITIONS
STRUCTURE

PYRAMID
WISDOM
LIFE KNOWLEDGE
MYSTERIES

QUEEN
PRESTIGE
SOPHISTICATION
MONARCHY

REAPER/DEATH
ENDINGS
LETTING
LIFE/DEATH CYCLE

ROPE
BINDING
RESTRICTIONS
TIED UP IN KNOTS

SACK/BAG
RESPONSIBILITIES
POSSESSIONS
WHAT IS CARRIED

SCALES
BALANCE
JUSTICE
FAIRNESS

 **SCROLL**
KNOWLEDGE
IMPORTANT INFORMATION
PASSING DOWN WISDOM

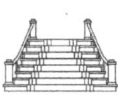 **STAIRS/STEPS**
PROGRESS
ASSISTANCE
STEP UP

 **SHIELD**
PROTECTION
DEFENSE
HONOR

 **SWORD**
MENTAL ASPECT
CUTTING THROUGH
HONOR

 **SHIP**
TRAVEL
JOURNEYS (WITHIN)
SHIP COMING IN

 **TOMB**
LAYING THINGS TO REST
LETTING GO OF THE OLD
FREEING STAGNANCY

 **SPHINX**
GUARDIAN
PROTECTOR OF SECRETS
CHALLENGES

 **UNICORN**
MAGIC
PURITY
UNIQUE

 **STAFF**
SUPPORT
DIRECTION
ASSISTS JOURNEYS

 **WAND**
MAGIC
MANIFESTING
CREATION

NATURE

 **BUTTERFLY**
CHANGE
NEW MINDSET
TRANSFORMATION

 **CLOUDS**
REVELATIONS
CLOUDED JUDGMENT
HIDDEN

 **BULL/OX**
POWER
STABILITY
RESISTANCE

 **CAT**
AWARENESS
PERCEPTION
INDEPENDENCE

 **BIRD**
FREEDOM
RISING UP
TAKING FLIGHT

 **DRAGONFLY**
TRANSFORMATION
POSITIVE CHANGE
SMOOTH PROCESS

DOG
LOYALTY
HONESTY
PROTECTION

FEATHER
DIVINE CONNECTIONS
CLEARING/CLEANSING
LIGHTNESS

DOVE
HOPE
PEACE
DIVINE MESSAGE

FISH
INTUITION
ABUNDANCE
SUBCONSCIOUS

DOWNWARD DOVE
HOLY SPIRIT
INNOCENCE
RECEIVING

GRAPES/VINES
ABUNDANCE
FERTILITY
REAPING HARVEST

ELEPHANT
MATRIARCHY
MATERNAL
WISDOM

GIRAFFE
STICKING YOUR NECK OUT
ACCEPTANCE
COMPASSION

FROG
SPIRIT REALM
TRANSITION
TRANSFORMATION

HORSE
MOVEMENT
VITALITY
GRACE

FALCON/HAWK/EAGLE
POWER
GRACE
SUPERIOR

ICE
PATIENCE
ISOLATION
CONTEMPLATION

FLOWERS
GROWTH
BEAUTY
ABUNDANCE

INSECT
PRODUCTIVITY
HIVE MIND
SCURRYING

FOX
QUICK ACTION
DECISIVENESS
OBSERVATION

IVY
WISDOM
PRESTIGE
HEALTH/LIFE

FIRE
ENERGY
PASSION
DESTRUCTION

LION
COURAGE
STRENGTH
AUTHORITY

 **LILY**
FERTILITY
PURITY
INNOCENCE

 **MORNING GLORY**
MORTALITY
UNREQUITED LOVE
ALTERED STATES

 **LIGHTENING**
CREATION
DESTRUCTION
SEVERITY

 **OWL**
WISDOM
SEEKING
INTROSPECTION

 **LIZARD**
RENEWAL
SMALL EFFORTS
REBIRTH

 **OCEAN**
DEPTH
UNSEEN POTENTIAL
POSSIBILITIES

 **LOTUS**
REGENERATION
TRANSFORMATION
RISING ABOVE

 **PLOUGHED FIELDS**
REAPING REWARDS
NURTURE PROSPECTS
EFFORT REQUIRED

 **LOBSTER/CRAYFISH**
REGENERATION
LIFE CYCLES
PROTECTION

 **PATH/ROADS**
DIRECTION
JOURNEY
TAKING STEPS

 **LAMB**
PURITY
INNOCENCE
BLESSING

 **POMEGRANATE**
BOUNTIFUL
PASSIONATE
PRESTIGE

 **MOON**
REFLECTION
INTUITION
HIDDEN WISDOM

 **PLANT**
GROWTH
LIFE GIVING
HEALTH

 **MOUNTAINS**
TRIUMPH
CHALLENGES
ENDURANCE

 **RAIN**
WASHING AWAY
CLEANSING
RENEWAL

 **MUSHROOM**
WISDOM
ALTERED STATE
SPIRIT REALM

 **RAM**
ACTION
LEADERSHIP
DETERMINATION

RABBIT/HARE
BOUNTIFUL
FERTILITY
BIRTH/LIFE

ROSE
PROMISE
BEAUTY
HONESTY

SNAKE
HEALTH
RENEWAL
SHEDDING

SNAIL
CAUTION
SECURITY
STEADY PROGRESS

STAR
DIRECTION
ILLUMINATION
DIVINE GUIDANCE

SUN
TRANSITION
GROWTH
LIFE FORCE

SUNFLOWER
LIGHT SIDE
GOOD OMENS
HAPPINESS

SNOW
ISOLATION
HARSH CONDITIONS
SECLUSION

SPIDER
WEAVING
CREATION
MANIFESTING

SCORPION
DEFENSE
TRANSFORMATION
SENSITIVITY

SQUIRREL
BUILDING RESERVES
PREPAREDNESS
OVER BUSY

TIGER
REGAL
DIGNIFIED
WILLPOWER

VOLCANO
FORCE
DESTRUCTION
UNPREDICTABLE

WEB
CREATION
CAUGHT UP
FEELING TRAPPED

WATERFALL
EMOTIONS
SUBCONSCIOUS
GOING WITH THE FLOW

WOLF
PRIMAL ASPECTS
INSTINCTS
INTELLIGENCE

WREATH
VICTORY
VALOR
TRIUMPH

ZEBRA
DUALITY
BALANCE
PERSPECTIVES

NUMBERS

ZERO
VOID/EMPTY
OPENNESS
POSSIBILITIES

ONE
CREATION
BEGINNING
INDEPENDENCE

TWO
CHOICES
DUALITY
BALANCE

THREE
PROGRESS
ADVANCEMENT
GROUP EFFORT

FOUR
GOALS
STABILITY
FOUNDATION

FIVE
GROWTH
CHALLENGES
UNPREDICTABLE

SIX
SAFETY
NURTURING
PROTECTION

SEVEN
KNOWLEDGE
AWARENESS
INTROSPECTION

EIGHT
PURPOSE
DECISIONS
OPPORTUNITIES

NINE
FULFILLMENT
ATTAINMENT
ACHIEVEMENT

SIGNS ✴ SYMBOLS ✴ GEOMETRY

AIR
THE MIND ASPECT
KNOWLEDGE
LEARNING

ALPHA
BEGINNING
ALL POWERFUL
ULTIMATE

ANARCHY
ABSENCE OF INSTITUTIONS
ULTIMATE FREEDOM
DISORDER WITH PURPOSE

ANKH
BALANCE
SYMBOL OF LIFE
IMMORTALITY

BAGUA
EIGHT AREAS OF LIFE
BALANCE OF ASPECTS
PRINCIPLES OF REALITY

CHAOS
DISORDER
CONFUSION
SPIN CYCLES

 **CADUCEUS**
HEALTH
WELLBEING
BALANCE

 **CIRCLE**
CYCLES
WHOLENESS
COMPLETION

 **CUBE**
STABILITY
PERMANENCE
PERFECTION

 **DEOSIL/DEISEAL**
SUN WARD
PROSPEROUS ROUTE
SIMPLER ROUTE

 **DODECAHEDRON**
GUIDANCE FROM THE DIVINE
SUBTLE ENERGIES OF SPIRIT
THE UNIVERSE

 **DREAM CATCHER**
SAFETY
TRANQUILITY
PROTECTION

 **EARTH**
STRUCTURE
FOUNDATION
STABILITY

 **EGG OF LIFE**
NEW LIFE
BEGINNINGS
FRESH STARTS

 **EYE OF HORUS**
POWER
ALL SEEING
THIRD EYE

 **EYE OF PROVIDENCE**
IN GODS CARE
DIVINE PROTECTION
PREPAREDNESS

 **EYE OF RA**
RADIANCE
ENLIGHTENMENT
PROTECTION

 **FAIRY STAR/SETAGRAM**
FAIRY REALMS
SACRED ITEMS
NUMBER SEVEN

 **FIRE**
CREATION
DESTRUCTION
PASSION

 **FLOWER OF LIFE**
DESIGN OF LIFE
EVERYTHING IN EXISTENCE
ULTIMATE CONNECTION

 **FRUIT OF LIFE**
UNIVERSAL BLUEPRINT
FINDING PURPOSE
FULFILLMENT

 **GUNGNIR**
POWER
PROTECTION
AUTHORITY

 **HEART**
LOVE
COMMITMENT
COMPASSION

 **HELM OF AWE**
VICTORY
PROTECTION
STRENGTH

HORNED GOD
NATURE
WILDERNESS
NATURAL INSTINCT

ICOSAHEDRON
TRUST IN UNIVERSE
UNIVERSAL KNOWLEDGE
EMOTIONAL ASPECT

LABYRINTH
WHOLENESS
JOURNEY TO CENTRE
PURPOSEFUL PATH

LEMNISCATE/INFINITY
POWERFUL
CONTINUITY
INFINITE ENERGY

MANDALA
CREATION
CONNECTION
COMPLETION

MERKABA
UNION ON ENERGIES
DUALITY
UNION WITH THE DIVINE

METATRONS CUBE
UNIVERSAL BALANCE
UNIVERSAL JOURNEY
PROGRESSION OF ENERGY

MJOLNIR
CREATE FROM DESTRUCTION
LIFE FORCE
POWER/STRENGTH

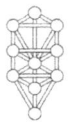
SEPHIROTIC TREE
CREATION
ASCENSION
JOURNEY

OCTAHEDRON
UNCONDITIONAL LOVE
COMPASSION
ACCEPTANCE

OMEGA
FINALITY
ENDINGS
POWER

OHM
UNIVERSE
WHOLENESS
UNITY

ODINS HORN
UNITY
CONNECTION
UNIVERSE

PEACE
PEACE
LOVE
UNITY

PENTAGRAM/PENTACLE
PROTECTION
PHYSICAL ASPECT
FIVE ELEMENTS

ROD OF ASCLEPIUS
HEALTH
HEALING
WELLBEING

SEED OF LIFE
FOUNDATION
BASE OF CREATION
GOD CONSCIOUSNESS

OUROBOROS
DESTRUCTION/REBIRTH
CYCLES OF LIFE
REGENERATION

64 TETRAHEDRON
HARMONY
STABILITY
UNION

TRIANGLE
INTELLIGENCE
ENERGY
UNION

SPIRAL GODDESS
DIVINE FEMININE
YIN ENERGY
LIFE CYCLES

TRIPLE CROSS
LIGHT
GOOD OMEN
BLESSING

SQUARE
ORDER
CONTAINMENT
STRUCTURE

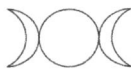
TRIPLE GODDESS
INTUITION
DIVINE FEMININE
YIN ENERGY

SHRI YANTRA
COSMIC CONNECTION
POTENTIAL
MANIFESTATION

TRIQUETRA
TRIPLE GODDESS ASPECT
FEMININITY
UNITY

STAR OF DAVID
UNITY
DUALITY
DIVINITY

TRISKELION
SYMMETRY
CREATION
DESTRUCTION

TEN COMMANDMENTS
MORAL CODE
ETHICS
ORDER

UMALOME
JOURNEY OF LIFE
TRANSFORMATION
LIFE/DEATH

TETRAHEDRON
STABILITY
BALANCE
CREATION

UNICURSAL HEXAGRAM
CONTINUITY
INFINITY
HARMONY

THUNDER CROSS
HEALTH
CREATION
PROSPERITY

VALKNUT
STRENGTH
HONOR
COURAGE

TREE OF LIFE
WISDOM
GROWTH
JOURNEY

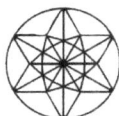
VECTOR EQUILIBRIUM
FORCES
EQUILIBRIUM
PERFECTION

 **VEGVISOR**
DIRECTION
INNER COMPASS
ASSISTANCE IN DARK TIMES

 **VESICA PISCIS**
CREATION
BALANCE
CONSCIOUSNESS

 **WATER**
EMOTIONS
INTUITION
NATURAL FLOW

 **WEB OF WYRD**
INTERCONNECTEDNESS
PAST, PRESENT, FUTURE
FATE/DESTINY

 **WHIDDERSHINS**
COUNTERING
HARDER PATH
COUNTER CLOCKWISE

 **YIN/YANG**
DUALITY
BALANCE
LIGHT/DARK

 **ZIA PUEBLA**
ENERGY
CREATION
LIFE FORCE

Chapter 13

Intuition Development

Intuition is an aspect of ourselves that we all possess. It is not something exclusive to a select few, but an innate ability that can be nurtured and strengthened. It is the ability to understand or comprehend something without using conscious thought. You just know. Intuition bypasses logical reasoning, but we use the conscious mind to assess and make sense of what our intuition is telling us.

Trust is the foundation for developing intuition. Without trust, intuitive messages can be missed, misinterpreted or ignored. Intuition is your inner compass, guide and teacher. You can sit with the most knowledgeable mentors in the world, but none will have the best or most accurate answers for you - only your intuition can provide that. If we break the word intuition down, we get in-tuition, meaning inner learning, which expresses the nature of intuition perfectly.

Everyone's intuition is different because it is shaped by personal experiences. Developing intuition is not about acquiring something new, but rather about reconnecting with what is already there. The more you use it, the stronger and clearer it becomes. However, receiving intuitive insights is only half the process - what you choose to do with them is what truly matters. Many people receive profound wisdom through Tarot, dreams or other intuitive channels, but fail to act on it because they do not trust themselves. Honoring your intuition means listening to it and acting accordingly. If trust is an issue, use the Tarot to explore why, but do not be afraid to look inward.

Recognizing Intuition

A common question is, how do I know it's my intuition? Many struggle to distinguish intuition from other mental voices such as fear, doubt, or over-analysis. Here are some key signs that intuition is speaking:

- You consistently feel uneasy about a situation or decision.
- A recurring thought or idea keeps surfacing throughout the day.
- Things feel, look, or sound clearer, even if they don't logically make sense.
- You just know, without doubt, that something is right.
- You feel confident in a decision that does not seem logical.

Fear, on the other hand, is often loud, urgent, and anxiety-inducing. Intuition is subtle and steady - it does not demand immediate action or create panic. Learning to recognize the difference between fear and intuition takes practice, but paying attention to how a message feels in the body can help. Fear feels heavy, tight, and restrictive, while intuition often feels expansive, light, and clear.

The Clairs — Our Intuitive Channels

Just as we have five physical senses, we also have inner-based senses known as the Clairs. These are the ways intuition communicates. Each person may have a dominant Clair or use a combination of them.

CLAIRVOYANCE	CLEAR SEEING
CLAIRAUDIENCE	CLEAR HEARING
CLAIRSENTIENCE	CLEAR FEELING
CLAIRCOGNIZANCE	CLEAR KNOWING
CLAIRALIENCE	CLEAR SMELL
CLAIRGUSTANCE	CLEAR TASTE

The Clairs

The more you work with intuition, the more you will notice which sense is strongest for you.

Other Intuitive Connections

- **Body Language** – Paying attention to non-verbal cues such as posture, facial expressions, and gestures can offer intuitive insight into others.
- **External Messages** – Intuition often speaks through unexpected channels, such as overheard conversations, repeated symbols, or meaningful coincidences.
- **Empathy** – Some people feel intuitive messages through their emotions or even physical sensations that are not their own. This is particularly common for those with strong empathic abilities.

Key Aspects of Intuition

- **Relax** – To clearly hear intuition, you need to be in a calm and receptive state. Stress, distraction, or overthinking can cloud intuitive messages. Creating space for stillness through meditation or quiet reflection helps open intuitive channels.
- **Tools** – Tarot, runes, pendulums, and other divination methods help bypass the critical mind and access intuition. Finding a tool that resonates can aid in development.
- **Awareness** – Developing intuition requires self-awareness. Practicing mindfulness and paying attention to thoughts, emotions, and subtle impressions helps strengthen intuitive perception.
- **Observation** – Approaching intuition with an observational mindset rather than jumping to conclusions reduces misinterpretation. Observing patterns, sym-

bols, and recurring themes helps refine intuitive accuracy.
- **Connection** – Strong intuition comes from a deep connection with yourself and the world around you. Strengthening your connection to your inner voice enhances intuitive clarity.

Daily Exercises

Gut Feel Exercise

Ask yourself simple questions and notice where you feel the answer in your body. Start with small choices like whether to have tea or coffee, and progress to deeper questions over time.

Sleep on It

Before bed, write down a question or area you need clarity on. Keep this intention in mind as you fall asleep. Upon waking, record any dreams, thoughts, or sudden insights. Intuitive messages often surface during sleep.

Use a Tool

Work with a divination tool such as Tarot or oracle cards daily. Draw a single card in the morning and reflect on how it relates to your day. Over time, patterns will emerge, reinforcing intuitive trust.

Journal Writing

Write about a topic without stopping to think. Let the words flow freely and reread them afterward. This form of automatic writing often brings forward intuitive insights.

Additional Exercises
Channeling

Sit in a quiet space where you won't be disturbed. Choose a method such as writing, speaking, or drawing and allow information to flow without forcing it. Let go of expectations and see what emerges.

Visualization Exercise

Imagine a long corridor with multiple doors. Walk down the corridor and choose a door that stands out. Step inside and explore what you see. This room holds the insight you need. This visualization helps bypass rational thought and access intuitive guidance.

30-Day Intuition Challenge

For those wanting a more structured practice, a simple 30-day challenge can be helpful. Commit to engaging in one intuitive exercise per day - whether it's pulling a Tarot card, observing synchronicities or practicing tuning in.

Do be mindful of doing too much work though! Yes, this is a real thing. As much as I recommend some long term commitment goals such as a 30-day challenge or a card-a-day, do take breaks in between. Be aware that you are channeling here and for those new to this don't quite realize the toll it takes on you physically, energetically and mentally. This is particularly true if you are doing intuitive development work or self-work.

Bringing it into Practice

- Pay attention to subtle nudges and impressions throughout the day.
- Trust the first answer that comes to mind instead of overthinking.
- Incorporate intuitive exercises into daily routines.
- Keep a record of intuitive experiences to track progress.
- Recognize that intuition is always present - it just needs to be listened to.

Developing intuition is a lifelong journey. The more you trust it, the more it will reveal. By integrating these practices, one can cultivate a deeper relationship with their inner knowing and enhance their ability to work with Tarot, spiritual practices and daily life with greater clarity.

Chapter 14

Oracle Cards

Oracle cards should not be confused with Tarot. While both can be used for divination and self-reflection, their structure and purpose differ significantly. Tarot follows a defined system of seventy-eight cards divided into the major and minor arcana, with consistent suits and a structured journey. Oracle cards, on the other hand, do not adhere to a standardized structure. Each deck is created with its own theme, number of cards and intended use, making them more fluid and flexible tools for insight.

One of the key differences between Tarot and Oracle cards is the depth and complexity of interpretation. Tarot provides a system that requires understanding relationships between cards, numerology and symbolic layers. Oracle decks tend to be more straightforward. Many offer direct messages or affirmations that can be interpreted at face value without requiring prior knowledge of a structured system. Because of this, Oracle decks are particularly useful when seeking quick insights or guidance that does not require the in-depth exploration that Tarot readings often demand.

Using Oracle Cards alongside Tarot

Oracle cards can be used alongside Tarot to enhance readings, offering additional clarity, reinforcement or a fresh perspective. While Tarot follows a structured system, Oracle cards provide intuitive, free-flowing guidance that can highlight key themes or add emphasis to specific messages.

They can be used at the beginning of a Tarot reading to establish an overall theme, helping to set the intention for the session. Drawing an Oracle card after a Tarot reading can provide a final takeaway, helping to summarize the most important insight or leaving the querent with a message to reflect on.

Some practitioners integrate Oracle cards within a Tarot spread, using them to clarify a particular card or situation. If a Tarot reading presents an ambiguous outcome or conflicting messages, an Oracle card can help break through uncertainty by providing a direct and simple answer.

Because Oracle decks are diverse in design and intent, they can be tailored to suit different reading styles and needs. They are particularly useful when seeking encouragement, affirmations or intuitive prompts that Tarot may not explicitly provide.

Choosing an Oracle Deck

Choosing the right Oracle deck depends on personal resonance, intention and the type of messages one seeks. Some Oracle decks function as simple messenger cards, providing brief yet powerful statements of guidance. An example of this is *Chris-*

Anne's Sacred Creators Oracle, which delivers direct and inspiring messages designed to inspire action and creativity.

Other Oracle decks are designed for a specific purpose, such as the *Moonology* deck, which aligns with lunar cycles and astrology to provide insight into timing and energy shifts. There are also variations of chakra decks that focus on balancing and understanding one's energetic system. Some decks incorporate a blend of visuals and messages, creating a deeper reflective experience. The *Work Your Light Oracle* and *Angels and Ancestors Oracle* are examples of this style, where the imagery is designed to evoke an intuitive response, supported by a guiding phrase or theme.

There are also Oracle decks that are strongly theme-based, appealing to specific spiritual or mythological traditions. These can include animal spirit decks that offer guidance through nature-based wisdom, fairy-themed decks that draw on folklore and elemental energy, or angelic Oracle decks that connect with messages of divine guidance. The diversity in Oracle decks means there is something for every style of practice, whether one seeks direct affirmations, spiritual depth or thematic guidance.

Selecting an Oracle deck should be an intuitive process, guided by what feels most aligned with one's practice. If working with Oracle cards alongside Tarot, it helps to choose a deck that complements one's reading style.

For those who prefer structure, a purpose-driven Oracle deck may provide the best fit, while those who rely on intuition may find decks with strong imagery and abstract messages to be more effective.

Experimenting with different Oracle decks allows one to refine their approach, discovering which types of messages resonate most and how best to incorporate them into readings.

Other Divination Tools that Integrate with Tarot

Oracle cards are not the only divination tools that can be used alongside Tarot. Many other practices complement Tarot readings, helping to deepen insight and provide additional layers of meaning.

Pendulums - These are often used to receive yes or no answers when clarity is needed. They can be particularly useful in Tarot readings when a direct confirmation or decision is required.

Runes - An ancient divination system using symbols carved into stones or wood, can be drawn in combination with Tarot to add extra depth to a reading. They offer a different symbolic language that can confirm or expand upon the message of a Tarot spread.

Astrology - Another complementary practice to align with the cards. Tarot readings can align with astrological cycles, using planetary transits and moon phases to determine timing and energetic influences. Some Tarot practitioners work with birth charts to provide highly personalized readings.

Scrying - Whether through a crystal ball, water or mirror, scrying can enhance intuitive insight. It allows one to work with the subconscious, much like Tarot, and can provide symbolic messages that add to a reading.

Each divination tool has its own strengths and integrating multiple tools into a practice allows for a more layered and comprehensive approach. Whether using Oracle cards, pendulums, astrology or other methods, the key is finding what resonates and supports intuitive work.

Oracle cards, with their flexible nature, are one of the easiest tools to work with alongside Tarot. Whether used on their own or as part of a larger reading, they offer valuable insight and guidance, making them a powerful addition to any divination practice.

About Tam Dillon

Tam Dillon is a self-development coach, mentor and published author with over 25 years of experience working with spiritual tools and practices. Her journey with spirituality began in her mid-teens, driven by a deep fascination with ancient teachings, divination and the nature of human consciousness. In the early 2000's she began offering professional readings and in 2007 offered her first course - The Art of Tarot. In 2011 she shifted to providing her offerings full-time and incorporate energy healing and crystals into her services.

Seeking broader experiences, Tam left her home country of South Africa and moved to Vietnam, where she settled in Hanoi. There, she opened a Tarot café in the city's Old Quarter, creating a welcoming space for spiritual seekers to explore Tarot and other esoteric practices. During this time, she explored Hanoi's vibrant Tarot scene and befriended some gifted Readers.

In 2019, she stepped away from professional Tarot readings, completed a mindfulness certification and transitioned into self-development coaching. She pursued further certifications in counseling, applied modern psychology and life and happiness coaching, gaining a well-rounded approach that integrates both ancient wisdom and contemporary psychology. After moving to the United States to join her husband, whom she met while living in Hanoi, she completed a 200-hour yoga teacher training, deepening her understanding of yogic philosophy and its connection to self-awareness.

Tam's approach to Tarot evolved leading her to develop the Yogic Tarot system over the span of three years from 2021. The system offers a unique integration of Tarot and yogic principles designed to offer deeper insights into self-development. This system has been compiled into a guidebook set for release later in 2025. At time of publishing, Tam is building out her informational content on her official YouTube channel to aid teaching the Yogic Tarot system and its associated poses.

Her self-development coaching guides clients in building resilience, cultivating clarity and embracing transformation. Her mentorship program supports naturally gifted healers, offering a space to explore their roles, understand their gifts and find direction in a modern context. She also offers Tarot Therapy sessions, blending intuitive insight with coaching to help clients identify patterns, personal roadblocks and areas of active growth.

Tam's mission is to empower individuals to take ownership of their personal and spiritual development, moving beyond quick-fix solutions toward sustainable, meaningful change. Through her coaching, mentorship, writing and free resources, she fosters a supportive environment where one can develop resilience, refine self-awareness and cultivate a deeper connection with their authentic self.

Tam Dillon
ACADEMY

WHERE ANCIENT WISDOM MEETS THE MODERN DAY SEEKER

Explore teachings that bridge tradition and practical living. The Tam Dillon Academy offers courses, books and education resources for self-development, tarot, yogic philosophy and more.

For those ready to grow beyond theory into living wisdom.

WWW.ACADEMY.TAMDILLON.COM

www.ingramcontent.com/pod-product-compliance
Lightning Source LLC
Chambersburg PA
CBHW061206070526
44583CB00025B/3140